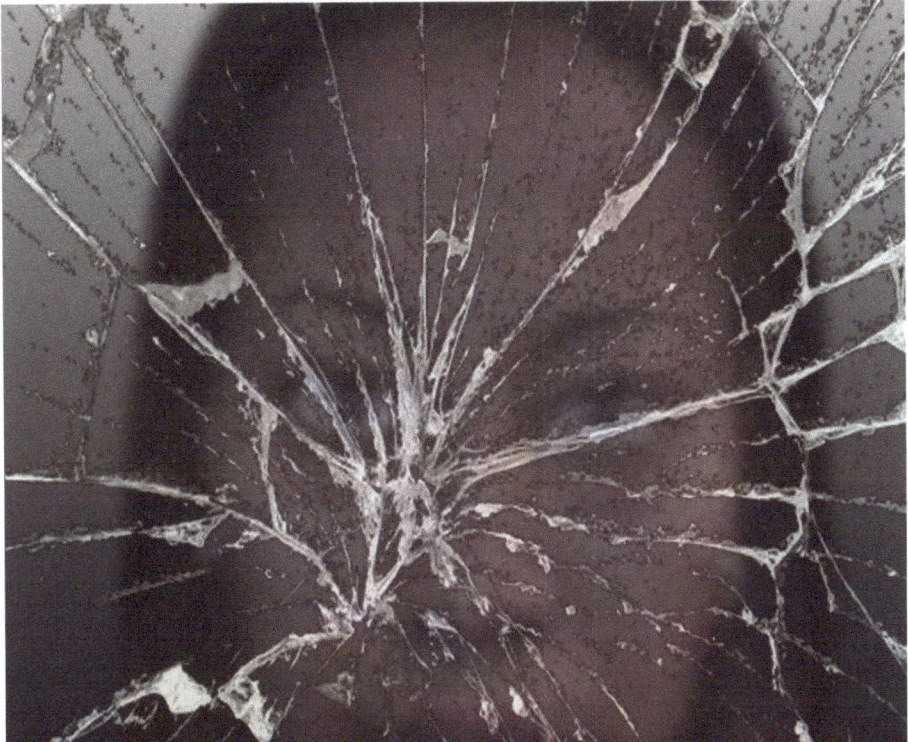

Unleashed Anger, Anger Unleashed is a work of non-fiction; however, names have been excluded to protect all involved parties.

All scripture are from the King James Version of the Holy Bible. All Scripture in italics are from the Amplified Version of the Holy Bible.

CLF Publishing, LLC.
9161 Sierra Ave, Ste. 203C
Fontana, CA 92335
www.clfpublishing.org

Reprinted in 2010- 2nd Edition (with minor changes).

Cover Design by Senir Design. Contact information- info@senirdesign.com.

ISBN# 978-0-9961971-4-4 (Set Free)
ISBN # 978-1-5997550-2-1(Unleashed Anger)

Printed in the United States of America.

Dedications

This book is dedicated to my three brothers: Noah A. Williams, Sr., Rodney D. Flemister, and August S. Harrison. Thank you for your everlasting love and support. Thanks for always having my back.

This poem is also dedicated to all three of you.

Brothers to a Sister

A brother's love comes in different degrees.
As a child, he'll help you scrape your knees.
By pushing you down and being a bit rough.
But he's only trying to make you tough.

Tough enough to withstand all you may engage in.
And when he becomes a teenager, he will help you win.
All your battles you have with boys.
And your brother will wish you still played with toys.

As you mature, he watches you.
And he doesn't know what he's going to do.
It's out of his control.
Because he can no longer grab hold.

Of the little girl you once were.
Because now you wear a dress, heels, and a fur.

And like wine, you get more precious with age.
And as a brother matures, he lets go of the rage.

And as he matures and steps back and gazes,
The expression on his face says he is amazed
At the creation he helped to form,
As he now extends out his arm.

To assist his sister with grace and finesse,
As he watches her while she's at her best.

Although brothers are close to our hearts,
They can be pesky and overbearing.
But that is just their way of showing
That they are protective, loving, and caring.

Acknowledgements

Special acknowledgements are sent to the following individuals who took time from their busy schedules to read my testimonial and give me the reviews that are printed on the back cover: Evangelist Marcella Flanagan, Evangelist Mary Jackson, Sis. Julia Lary, and Katherine Young. Their heartfelt comments added insight and momentum to this project.

Much love and gratitude to each of you.

Unleashed Anger, Anger Unleashed

Prologue

Unleashed Anger, Anger Unleashed was birthed out of my desire to be set free from my anger-filled condition, which has thirty-three year old roots.

The various chapters in the book represent the stages that I went through during my transformation. Similar to the writing process (which has several steps), healing is not a lateral or hierarchical process. Rather, I found it to be a recursive process, meaning that a person does not simply pass from one stage to the next conquering each stage as he/she goes. Instead, each stage may be visited more than once in order for the entire process to be effective.

As you peruse the pages of this book and explore your transformation (if this is your purpose for reading), be sure to visit and revisit each stage of the process for as long as you feel necessary. I found that healing cannot be rushed, but it definitely can be prolonged. So before you begin the healing process you must decide if you truly want to be delivered from a condition that damages your life as well as the lives of others. Once your mind is made up don't let anyone change it or make you believe that God is not powerful enough to come in and change the heart and mindset of a willing vessel.

I pray God's many blessings upon you as you press forward and take on the challenge of being healed and set free. Remember, you only have one opponent- Satan, but even he and his army must bow to the name of our Lord and Savior, Jesus Christ.

Dr. Cassundra White-Elliott

Table of Contents

PART
ONE

IT'S NEVER WHAT YOU THINK!

Introduction

What Is This Book All About?

As I prepared to embark upon the adventure of writing this book, I had to prepare myself to also be transparent. I have found that being transparent is required in order for healing to transpire, healing for all those that peruse the pages of this book and myself. And I may as well tell you that today, at the onset of this project, I have not been totally delivered from my condition of being an anger-filled person. However, I am definitely a work in progress. I have made strides with the assistance of my Lord and Savior, Jesus Christ, who is the head of my life. Without his love, guidance, and teachings, I would not be the woman of God I am today. I shudder to think where I could be instead and will therefore not entertain the thought.

Rather, I will confess that it is my desire that a transformation will result as I do an in-depth exploration of who I started out as when I was a little girl, the woman I became, and the woman that I am striving to be. It is my endeavor to see God tear down walls that encapsulate both my mind and soul and free me from the bondages of anger. It is my prayer that total deliverance will come between the writing of this sentence and the very last one of the book.

So, it is at this point that I must stop and utter a word of prayer.

Oh Heavenly Father,
I just want to stop and take another moment to give you praise, honor, and glory for being just who you are. You are the Alpha and the Omega. You are the finisher of my faith, for you knew my beginning before I departed from my mother's womb and you know my ending as well. Father God, I just want to thank you for your grace, the grace that you have afforded me, oh Lord, to still be here and to be able to tell my story. A story that will set captives free, present company included. Father God, I just want to tell you that I love you because you love me in spite of me. You love me with all my imperfections. You love me because as it says in your word that I am a royal priesthood. I am the daughter of the Most High God; I am the daughter of the King of Kings. Father God, I thank you for your love and the strength to be able to cause this work to come to manifestation. Oh Lord Father, I humble in your sight. I place my face to the ground and cry out your name. I cry out for healing in the name of my Lord and Savior, Jesus Christ. I believe that you will give me favor and grace to heal and to let your glory reign mightily in my life. So, therefore I place my life back into your hands, so that you can do a mighty work. I enter this prayer in the name of your son, Jesus Christ.
Amen.

Readers, as the writing of this book takes me through my transformation, I pray that the reading and re-reading of it will take you through yours. If you desire to be free, as I do, remember freedom can be yours. It is a gift for believers of the Almighty God. We just need to first believe that we can be free, pray for freedom, receive our freedom (by the necessary path as revealed to us by the Holy Spirit), and then confess with our mouths that we are free and are no longer bound.

The next several chapters of the book will exemplify my testimony. However, in order to get to the issue at hand- being free from anger- each event that serves as a block in the total wall of anger will not be fully explored. A full explanation of each event will come later in my autobiography titled *From Despair, Through Desperation, to Victory*. Also, in order to not point the finger of blame for my actions to others, I will focus on my actions and pinpoint my detrimental behavior and the need and desire to be free and walk upright before the Lord.

Before delving into my testimony, let me provide you with scripture that you will find helpful in dealing with anger, as I did. First, though, we must understand that the anger that you are experiencing may stem from unforgiveness. If that is the case, and you have yet to forgive someone who has wronged you, then with forgiveness is where you must start in order to begin on your path of freedom. For others, we may have already forgiven our wrongdoers but not before the roots of anger had begun to form. Once anger takes root, it has to be excavated by the root and not simply by cutting off limb by limb. So, for whatever situation you face, the following scriptures will exemplify where God stands on unforgiveness and anger. Take a moment to read through them and feel free to read them again whenever you feel it necessary.

Also notice that after each King's James Version of the scripture, there is a translated version of each verse (*in italics*), which is taken from the New International Version and will provide more clarity of what God is saying to us.

Further, I will be the first to admit that even though we know the scriptures and can find peace in the Word of God, it is not automatic that because we know that acting out in anger is contrary to God's Word that we are able to control our tempers after a simple reading. It definitely takes an impartation of the Holy Spirit to make a difference in our behavior, but only if we are first willing and ask God's assistance in our transformation. So, be patient with yourself and take one step at a time.

<u>Forgiving Others</u>

Isaiah 43: 18-19

Remember ye not the former things, neither consider the things of old.

Behold, I will do a new thing; now it shall spring forth; shall ye not know it? I will even make a way in the wilderness, and rivers in the desert.

(Forget the former things; do not dwell on the past.

See, I am doing a new thing! Now it springs up; do you not perceive it? I am making a way in the desert and streams in the wasteland.)

Matthew 5:10-12

Blessed are they which are persecuted for righteousness' sake: for theirs is the kingdom of heaven.

Blessed are ye, when men shall revile you, and persecute you, and shall say all manner of evil against you falsely, for my sake.

Rejoice, and be exceedingly glad: for great is your reward in heaven: for so persecuted they the prophets which were before you.

(Blessed are those who are persecuted because of righteousness, for theirs is the kingdom of heaven.

Blessed are you when people insult you, persecute you and falsely say all kinds of evil against you because of me.

Rejoice and be glad, because great is your reward in heaven, for in the same way they persecuted the prophets who were before you.)

Matthew 5:44

But I say unto you, Love your enemies, bless them that curse you, do good to them that hate you, and pray for them which despitefully use you, and persecute you;

(But I tell you: Love your enemies and pray for those who persecute you,)

Matthew 6:14-15

For if ye forgive men their trespasses, your heavenly Father will also forgive you:

But if ye forgive not men their trespasses, neither will your Father forgive your trespasses.

(For if you forgive men when they sin against you, your heavenly Father will also forgive you.

But if you do not forgive men their sins, your Father will not forgive your sins.)

Matthew 18: 21-22

Then came Peter to him, and said, Lord, how oft shall my brother sin against me, and I forgive him? till seven times?

Jesus saith unto him, I say not unto thee, Until seven times: but, Until seventy times seven.

(Then Peter came to Him and said, "Lord, how often shall my brother sin against me, and I forgive him? Up to seven times?"

Jesus answered, "I tell you, not seven times, but up to seventy times seven.")

Mark 11:25

And when ye stand praying, forgive, if ye have aught against any: that your Father also which is in heaven may forgive you your trespasses.

(And when you stand praying, if you have anything against anyone, forgive him, so that your Father in heaven may forgive your sins.)

Luke 17:3

Take heed to yourselves: If thy brother trespass against thee, rebuke him; and if he repent, forgive him.

(Take watch yourselves. If your brother sins, rebuke him; and if he repents, forgive him.)

Romans 12:21
Be not overcome of evil, but overcome evil with good.
(Do not be overcome by evil, but overcome evil with good.)

Ephesians 4:31-32
Let all bitterness, and wrath, and anger, and clamour, and evil speaking, be put away from you, with all malice:
And be ye kind one to another, tenderhearted, forgiving one another, even as God for Christ's sake hath forgiven you.
(Get rid of all bitterness, rage, and anger, brawling and slander, along with every for of malice.
Be kind and compassionate to one another, forgiving each other, just as in Christ God forgave you.)

Philippians 3:13-14
Brethen, I count not myself to have apprehended: but this one thing I do, forgetting those things, which are behind, and reaching forth unto those things, which are before,
I press toward the mark for the prize of the high calling of God in Christ Jesus.
(Brothers, I do not consider myself yet to have taken hold of it. But one thing I do, Forgetting what is behind and straining toward what is ahead,
I press on toward the goal to win the prize for which God has called me heavenward in Christ Jesus.)

Colossians 3:13
Forbearing one another, and forgiving one another, if any man have a quarrel against any: even as Christ forgave you, so also do ye.
(Bear with each other and forgive whatever grievances you may have against one another. Forgive as the Lord forgave you.)

Hebrews 10:30

For we know him that hath said, Vengeance belongeth unto me, I will recompense, saith the Lord. And again, The Lord shall judge his people.

(For we know him who said, "It is mine to avenge, I will repay," and again, "The Lord will judge his people.")

I Peter 2: 19-23

For this is thankworthy, if a man for conscience toward God endure grief, suffering wrongfully.

For what glory is it, if, when ye be buffeted for your faults, ye shall take it patiently? but if, when ye do well, and suffer for it, ye take it patiently, this is acceptable with God.

For even hereunto were ye called: because Christ also suffered for us, leaving us an example, that ye should follow his steps:

Who did no sin, neither was guile found in his mouth:

Who, when he was reviled, reviled not again; when he suffered, he threatened not; but committed himself to him that judgeth righteously:

(For it is commendable if a man bears up under the pain of unjust suffering because he is conscious of God.

But how is it to your credit if you receive a beating for doing wrong and endure it? But if you suffer for doing good and you endure it, this is commendable before God.

To this you were called, because Christ suffered for you, leaving you an example, that you should follow in his steps.

He committed no sin, and no deceit was found in his mouth.

When they hurled their insults at him, he did not retaliate; when he suffered, he made no threats. Instead, he entrusted himself to him who judges justly.

I Peter 3:9-10

Not rendering evil for evil, or railing for railing: but contrariwise blessing; knowing that ye are thereunto called, that ye should inherit a blessing.

For he that will love life, and see good days, let him refrain his tongue from evil, and his lips that speak no guile:

(Do not repay evil with evil or insult with insult, but with blessing, because to this you were called so that you may inherit a blessing.

For, "Whoever would love life and see good days must keep his tongue from evil and his lips from deceitful speech.)

I Peter 4:12-14

Beloved, think it not strange concerning the fiery trial which is to try you, as though some strange thing happened unto you:

But rejoice, inasmuch as ye are partakers of Christ's sufferings; that, when his glory shall be revealed, ye may be glad also with exceeding joy.

If ye be reproached for the name of Christ, happy are ye; for the spirit of glory and of God resteth upon you: on their part he is evil spoken of, but on your part he is glorified.

(Dear friends, do not be surprised at the painful trail you are suffering, as though something strange were happening to you,

But rejoice that you participate in the sufferings of Christ, so that you may be overjoyed when his glory is revealed.

If you are insulted because of the name of Christ, you are blessed, for the Spirit of glory and of God rests on you.)

Releasing Anger

Psalms 37:8

Cease from anger, and forsake wrath: fret not thyself in any wise to do evil.

(Refrain from anger and turn from wrath; do not fret- it leads only to evil.)

Proverbs 14:16-17

A wise man feareth, and departeth from evil: but the fool rageth, and is confident.

He that is soon angry dealeth foolishly: and a man of wicked devices is hated.

(A wise man fears the Lord and shuns evil, but a fool is hotheaded and reckless.

A quick-tempered man does foolish things, and a crafty man is hated.)

Proverbs 14:29

He that is slow to wrath is of great understanding: but he that is hasty of spirit exalteth folly.

(A patient man has great understanding, but a quick-tempered man displays folly.)

Proverbs 15:1

A soft answer turneth away wrath: but grievous words stir up anger.

(A gentle answer turns away wrath, but a harsh word stirs up anger.)

Proverbs 16:32

He that is slow to anger is better than the mighty; and he that ruleth his spirit than he that taketh a city.

(Better a patient man than a warrior, a man who controls his temper than one who takes a city.)

Proverbs 25:21-22

If thine enemy be hungry, give him bread to eat: and if he be thirsty, give him water to drink:

For thou shalt heap coals of fire upon his head, and the Lord shall reward thee.

(If your enemy is hungry, give him food to eat; if he is thirsty, give him water to drink.

In doing this, you will heap burning coals on his head, and the Lord will reward you.)

Ecclesiastes 7:9

Be not hasty in thy spirit to be angry: for anger resteth in the bosom of fools.

(Do not be quickly provoked in your spirit, for anger resides in the lap of fools.)

Matthew 5:22-24

But I say unto you, That whosoever is angry with his brother without a cause shall be in danger of the judgment: and whosoever shall say to his brother, Ra'-ca, shall be in danger of the council: but whosoever shall say, Thou fool, shall be in danger of hell fire.

Therefore if thou bring thy gift to the altar, and there rememberest that thy brother hath ought against thee;

Leave there thy gift before the alter, and go thy way; first be reconciled to thy brother, and then come and offer thy gift.

(But I tell you anyone who is angry with his brother will be subject to judgment. Again, anyone who says to his brother, Ra'-ca, is answerable to the Sanhedrin. But anyone who says, 'You fool!' will be in danger of the fire of hell.

Therefore, if you are offering your gift at the altar and there remember that your brother has something against you,

Leave your gift there in front of the altar. First go and be reconciled to your brother; then come and offer your gift.)

Matthew 6:14

For if ye forgive men their trespasses, your heavenly Father will also forgive you:

(For if you forgive men when they sin against you, your heavenly Father will also forgive you.)

Romans 12:19

Dearly beloved, avenge not yourselves, but rather give place unto wrath: for it is written, Vengeance is mine; I will repay, saith the Lord.

((Do not take revenge, my friends, but leave room for God's wrath, for it is written: "It is mine to avenge; I will repay," says the Lord.)

Ephesians 4:26

Be ye angry, and sin not: let not the sun go down upon your wrath:

("In your anger do not sin:" Do not let the sun go down while you are still angry,)

Ephesians 4:31-32

Let all bitterness, and wrath, and anger, and clamour, and evil speaking, be put away from you, with all malice:

And be ye kind one to another, tenderhearted, forgiving one another, even as God for Christ's sake hath forgiven you.

(Get rid of all bitterness, rage, and anger, brawling and slander, along with every for of malice.

Be kind and compassionate to one another, forgiving each other, just as in Christ God forgave you.)

Colossians 3:8
But now ye also put off all these; anger, wrath, malice, blasphemy, filthy communication out of your mouth.
(But now you must rid yourself of all such things as these: anger, rage, malice, slander, and filthy language from your lips.)

Hebrews 10:30
For we know him that hath said, Vengeance belongeth unto me, I will recompense, saith the Lord. And again, the Lord shall judge his people.
(For we know him who said, "It is mine to avenge; I will repay," and again, "The Lord will judge his people.)

James 1:19-20
Wherefore, my beloved brethren, let every man be swift to hear, slow to speak, slow to wrath:
For the wrath of man worketh not the righteousness of a God.
(My dear brothers, take note of this: Everyone should be quick to listen, slow to speak, and slow to become angry,
For man's anger does not bring about the righteous life that God desires.)

Times of Innocence

How It All Started

As a little girl, I was joyful and fun-loving. I loved to talk to everyone and always had a story to tell or a question to ask. I enjoyed life with my mother and brothers, but that would soon be changed. From the age of four until the age of eleven, deception was being put into place. I experienced several incidents of molestation from close family members; the first remembrance of such an incident occurred at age four.

However, at the age of eleven, the onset of continued abuse became a part of my everyday life from a man that I had already despised because of his treatment of my brothers and me. He was my stepfather. Thankfully, before the situation could escalate further, my mother and he were divorced. Not because of me, but because of her own problems, for she did not know about me. She did not know because I did not tell her, as I was instructed. Also, I guess I expected her to know since she was my protector and provider.

Although my mother's divorce freed me from the abuse, it did not come before hatred, anger, and bitterness set in. This was the beginning of the change.

But let's take a step back, back to a time that existed before I was eleven. Between the age of four and eleven, many great things happened. I discovered my love for the art of teaching, reading, writing, and especially, math, all of which were nourished by my mother and my elementary school teachers.

Even though my mother was not omniscient nor the savior I expected her to be, due to my immature belief, she was a very good mother. She took good care of my brothers and me, throughout her divorce from my father and my stepfather and throughout her plight as a single mother of three sons and a daughter. She always encouraged me to strive to be all that I desire to be, and she still does.

While in school, I excelled in my studies and was very enthusiastic about school and learning. At the end of each school year, I always brought home the left over worksheets and all the books that the teachers were moving off the shelves to make room for the new ones. My mother rarely complained about me bringing all the extraneous papers home, but when she did, I would convince her that I needed each and every sheet of paper. Even at that age, I had a system of being organized, so I would have the worksheets arranged in a systematic fashion. Then, each summer, I subjected my brothers to summer school. I was the teacher and they were my students.

For the most part, I had a normal childhood. However, that was limited because my stepfather had strange rules, like not letting us outside to play with the neighborhood kids. We were permitted, however, to go outside on Saturday mornings to pick up the leaves that had fallen from the humongous tree that covered our entire front yard and hovered over the garage. The worst part about picking up the leaves from the yard is that our yard was filled with decorative rocks and we had to get the leaves from between the rocks. Some may say it built character or some other necessary trait, but I say it gave me hangnails on my fingers and made me feel like a slave.

Our lifestyle was so different from the other kids that we were labeled as outcasts and different. That didn't change until my mother was divorced and we were older and were then permitted to do what "normal" kids do- hang out with other kids.

After the episodes with my stepfather, one would think that maybe my life would return to normal. That couldn't be farther from the truth. At the age of fourteen (still a virgin), I was raped by a neighborhood boy and became pregnant. I was then told by my mother and doctor that I would have an abortion. Living the sheltered life that I had lived for fourteen years, I didn't quite understand. I simply knew that after the procedure that I would no longer be pregnant which I never fully understood that I was until my mother took me to the doctor after having spells of vomiting. I never experienced the life growing inside of me. The experience was over just as soon as it began. I never felt a loss or the pain of not having my unborn child. It was just a stolen moment in time.

Warning Signs

Bouts of Anger

If someone had been watching me, the warning signs that showed what were being manifested and taking root inside of me would have been detected. Looking back over my life with a sort of magnifying glass mentality, I see a pattern of destructive behavior. Actually, it is not even at this moment that I finally realized what had transpired; rather, I knew years ago what my issue was. Only I didn't know that it was this deep. What I did realize, however, is that I didn't care that I had an issue of having a hardcore attitude that was produced by the anger that I held within.

Following is a list of various incidents that transpired throughout my life at various intervals, over a 20-year period. They have been purposefully listed out of order of occurrence and without names of the other involved party in order to protect the identity of other individuals. One thing I will divulge is that all exemplified encounters involved men.

Incident #1 Deadly Weapon Assault
One day while getting my hair done, a police officer was going up and down the street that I was parked on, issuing tickets because the street did not allow parking after 3pm. It was five after three and my hair was not yet done. After approaching the officer, he told me to move my car or either he was going to

issue me a citation and then, he threatened to have it towed. After entering my vehicle, I proceeded to move my car into the back parking lot and suddenly the officer appeared in front of my car. As he banged on the hood, he yelled some words I couldn't understand. Becoming irritated by his belligerent attitude, I proceeded towards the back parking lot. On the way, I hit his leg with my car. As a result, I was charged with assault with a deadly weapon which was later reduced to a charge of dry reckless driving.

Incident #2 Trouble with the Boss

During my brief employment as an accounting clerk, I requested the morning off to go to a doctor's appointment because the appointment day and time that was offered to me was the only one that was available for a long time to come. When I requested the morning off, my boss told me that I could not be excused. I immediately became upset and called the district office to speak with his boss. His boss took the liberty to tell me that I could not be denied the right to have needed medical services, after I explained that I stay late when I'm asked to and I take work home when I need to keep the company's accounts in order and bills paid on time. After talking with my boss' boss, I took the liberty of attending my appointment.

When I returned to work, I was written up. Again, I called and voiced my opinion to the controller (my boss' boss). As a result of my complaint, a meeting was scheduled. At the meeting, I was surprised to find that they had decided to find some dirt on me. But the only thing that they could find was some days when I came in late. In the meeting, they admitted that I had the right to go to the doctor, but I needed to be on time to work.

I felt they were doing a splendid job of being controlling and misusing their power, like the cop in the above account. So, I proceeded to tell them that I was not wrong about my actions and that I believed that they were being controlling and attempting to keep me under their thumb, a place that I did not belong. I also added that if they had a problem with my conduct that they could fire me as a result. Of course they did not need my permission to fire me, but in the end they did not.

Incident #3 The Refrigerator Incident
After believing that I had been verbally threatened, the person who allegedly issued the threat was bending over looking in an office-size refrigerator. I politely walked over and kicked the refrigerator door shut, slamming his head inside. I offered a verbal explanation of my action by declaring that I did not appreciate being threatened and said that if anyone was going to get hurt it would not be me.

Incident #4 Telephone Connection
As a teenage girl, growing up with three brothers wasn't always the easiest thing to do. As it was one of my brothers' favorite pastimes to bother me, he went about his daily activity of working my last nerve. Well, on that day I wasn't in the mood to be bothered nor bullied for that matter. So, as I was trying to use the phone and he continued to torment me, I hit him upside his head with the phone in order to get him away from me.

Incident #5 Hand-to-Jaw Connection
Here we have the case of guy tries to use girl. Well, at least at the time that was my perception of the situation with an ex-boyfriend. After having a heated argument, I figured that I would have the last word. So after I finished yelling at him for

whatever it was that I was mad about, I socked him in his jaw and without blinking an eye, I walked away.

After all the accounts of my inexcusable behavior, I am extremely blessed on two counts. First, I am blessed because any one of the above accounts could have landed me in jail, the hospital, or the grave. So, I thank God for his grace and mercy. Secondly, I am blessed because God gave me further grace to come to a time of repentance, forgiveness, and healing.

Not only did I exhibit physical violence from time to time, I would verbally explode as well. However, as time goes on, I try to tame a virtually untamable member of my body: my tongue. The following poem exemplifies my desire to be freed from having good and evil exude from the same orifice.

Anger-Filled Words

No matter how near or far, everyone has a story to tell.
When speaking, the hurts and pains are found to dwell.
Deep inside hearts and minds, disappointments can be found.
Oh those things that easily beset us seem to abound.

On every hand and on every turn,
The words that wait to cross our lips seem to burn.
We try to hold them in, but they come flooding out.
Anytime we give them the opportunity when we scream and shout.

How is it that the tongue can coat but in the next moment slice?

How can a sweet and kind person instantly be colored no-so-nice?
All of these are strongholds and devices of the enemy.
But never fear, the heavenly Father has the perfect remedy.

If we seek Him in all that we do,
And remember the race is not given to the swift, but to me and you.
Those who demonstrate patience, control, endurance, long-suffering, willingness, love, and temperance.

But how can we gain and retain these personality traits?
Or is leading an anger-filled existence our destined fate?
Having us to believe that is yet another trick of the fallen one.
Instead, we should always continue to look and trust in the Father, Holy Spirit, and Son.

For the trinity has governance over our lives.
And for Them we should sacrifice.
And strive to be in a better state than we currently may be.
And not until then will we be set free.

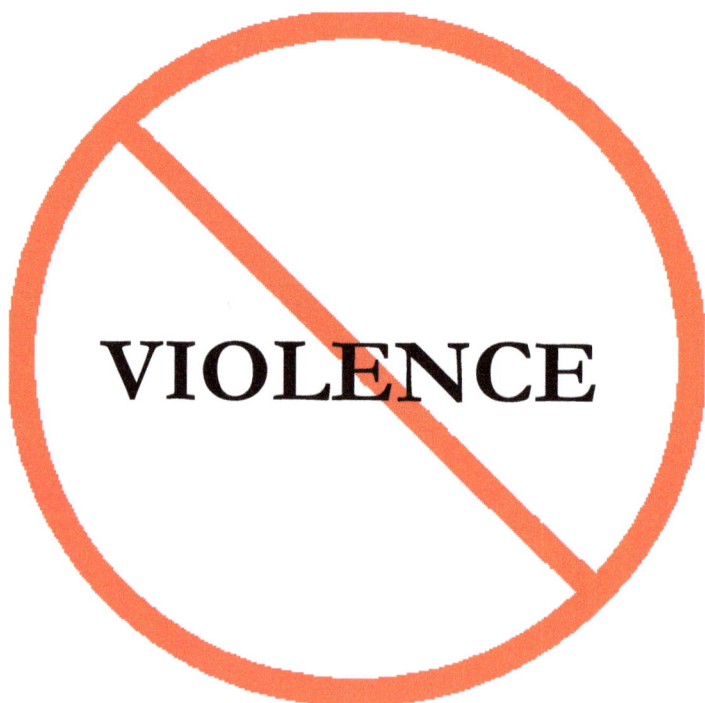

Self-Reflection

A Look in the Mirror

At this point in my life, I had to stop and do a self-reflection. I had to ask myself if I wanted to continue on the path of destruction that was becoming increasingly worse or if I wanted something better for those who come in contact with me and for myself as well. For the last few years, after an increase in individual episodes, I kept saying that I did not want to be a hurtful person and that I wanted to change. But I thought that just confessing that I wanted to change was enough. I found out years later that this is indeed not enough. I had to do something else in order for total deliverance to begin to come into manifestation. But before moving toward that stage, a change had to be made in my heart.

As I looked back over the events and recognized a destructive pattern, I began to feel remorse about my violent, rebellious behavior. However, during the actual occurrence of these events, I did not feel remorse because I felt justified in my actions. I believed that my victims deserved whatever happened to them because I felt that I was being victimized at the time and that I needed to defend myself against my attackers. But, I also had to realize that the truth is the truth no matter who gives their version of it. So regardless of what happened to me at the hands or mouths or attitudes of others and regardless of whether they do actually need to be punished for their behavior or if my thinking was tainted due to past experiences, the Bible says in Hebrews 10:30, "For we know him that hath said, Vengeance belongeth unto me, I will recompense, saith the Lord. And again, The Lord shall judge his people." So, if we are living by the Word, then we must also believe the Word has the last word and we must be willing to totally surrender to it. But I know, easier said than done right? Right.

So, what do we do when we find it difficult to adhere to the commandments that God has given to us in His word, in regards to anger and forgiveness? At this juncture, I believe it is appropriate to take time to reflect on what letting the Word have the last word means. But for now, let's do a self-reflection of who we are and who we desire to be. Then, we will return back to the above questions in the chapter, "Where Do We Go From Here?"

As we are taking a pause to do a self-reflection of the person that each of us is, read the following poems that I wrote during moments of frustration, relaxation, or venting. Through writing, I am able to release the feelings of anxiety and frustration. Also, I find that it helps me to focus and calm down. I am sharing these poems with you now because reading them can serve the same purposes for you that writing them did for me. After reading the poems, you may want to take a moment and write your own poem, song, jingle, or story. Even if being creative in writing is not your forte, it can be used as an outlet. And remember, no one has to see it. It can be used as an avenue to express your inner most feelings. This is what my poems do for me, while others use journals, diaries, mini cassette recorders, etc.

But remember, whatever you choose, make sure it is healthy for you and that it does not cause any more pain or incite violence within you. If you find that the activity causes you to be upset, refrain from being involved in it because to some degree you are focusing on the issue. However, later revisit the topic and see if you can ascertain the reason(s) for the rise in anger. Then, address it. Addressing the issue could mean having an open discussion with someone, praying to God, or doing deeper self-reflection and allowing the Holy Spirit room to reveal to you the mode of therapy you need to take.

As you read the poems on the next several pages, see if you can find yourself in them. Examine how they make you feel. They may tell you something about your level of self-esteem, your moods, and your fears, how you deal with unresolved issues, or even reveal where you are in the process of healing.

<u>Who Are You?</u>

When people see you, what do you want them to see?
What should the determinants be?

Do you want them to determine who you are
By characteristics such as gender, race, and creed, or something
more meaningful by far?

Although these characteristics are part of you,
They don't define your self-worth or the things you do.

How do you feel when people think you fit a specific
stereotype?
What are their assumptions based on, a scientific prototype?

What you have done and have potential to do
Should be the important things that speak for you.

Don't let the world's prejudices bring you down.
Wear a smile on your face instead of a frown.

Work hard to achieve your goals as you experience life.
And don't let others make you sacrifice.

Or give up your dreams, your self-esteem, or your hopes.
Stand tall and proud and remember to cope.

With a world full of prejudices and regrets,
Remember who you are in spite of it.

<u>Trepidation</u>
(Fear)

Fear is a common element that encompasses our souls.
It carefully moves around our hearts and slowly grabs hold.

It prevents you from moving out of your comfort zone
And the vast area that is set before you, you dare not roam.

Fear tramples your motivations and desires.
It is the ultimate quencher of all internal fires.

If this negative spirit prolongs inside your heart,
A cancer-like sore will have its start.

Fear is as debilitating as a handicap.
Turn your fear into something constructive, like a map.

A map that will direct you anywhere you want to go
To places where you can feel comfortable letting your feelings
flow.

Be positive and release that stronghold.
Without fear your true talents will begin to unfold.
And remember, regardless of what you hear,
God has not given us the spirit of fear.

Don't Look Back

In life, we all tend to make errors
But does that mean we need to live in constant terror?

Of continuously making mistakes
Or is it another chance we should take

If we live a life of constantly looking into the past,
What chance of a future do we have?

We can't go back and undo the dirt.
Regardless of how much we hurt.

The past is to be learned from.
To help in the experiences that will surely come.

Life is full of experiences that we live to tell.
What we learn is important and not the fact that we fell.

As we continue to learn, mature, and grow,
We can share with others all that we know.

So don't be down on yourself and stop looking back into the
past.
Look to a brighter future and a lot longer you'll last.

Disappointment

Life can sometimes send you for a loop that you never saw
coming.
And the unexpected change of events is almost enough to send
a person running.

But the best thing to do in this trying time of uncertainty
Is to walk boldly with your head uplifted and to think positively.

Try to keep focused and search for the good in the situation.
And if you pray and stand firm you may have an epiphany or a
revelation.

Staying focused and not giving in to the multitude of depressive
thoughts,
Will keep your mind clear from being strained and overwrought.

Disappointment is an emotion that can prevent you from
feeling free.
It may lead to bitterness and hatred, which are iniquities.

Express your feelings openly and calmly and you will see,
That your disappointment will begin to fade but maybe not
eternally.

For disappointment is a part of life that you will experience time
and time again.
But if you learn to maneuver through the ride, you will
eventually develop thicker skin.

This armour will help you to have a healthy outlook on life.

Because the disappointments will not be able to cause you undue stress and strife.

Feeling Provoked?

Don't Give In

"Put on the whole armour of God, that ye may be able to stand against the wiles of the devil."
Ephesians 6:11

Let's now take a direct look at the emotion that has been indirectly discussed for the last few chapters. We have discovered one way for anger to manifest, and we have surveyed some of the various episodes that can result from anger. Now let's explore what the specialists say about anger and how to control it before it consumes and/or controls us.

> Anger is a completely normal, usually healthy, human emotion. But when it gets out of control and turns destructive, it can lead to problems—problems at work, in your personal relationships, and in the overall quality of your life. And it can make you feel as though you're at the mercy of an unpredictable and powerful emotion. (APA par. 2)

"According to Charles Spielberger, PhD, a psychologist that specializes in anger, Anger is 'an emotional state that varies in intensity from mild irritation to intense fury and rage'" (APA par. 3).

Have you ever experienced being provoked to violence? You are not alone; many people will admit that at one time or another that they felt angered or enraged by someone's words or behavior. But, what have you noticed that is different about your response and the response of others? For me, I would say that some of my responses have even been explosive. Why is it that some people just seem to rub us the wrong way? Why is it that a particular person can say or do something that bothers you or gets under your skin, but if someone else said or did the same thing you wouldn't be bothered nearly as much, if at all? Why does is it appear that some people sometimes does it purposefully? Why is it that we want to lash out at them for their perceived behavior?

Although all of these questions appear to be important, none of them are as important as the next statement. **What others do or don't do should not have enough power to provoke us to engage in violent behavior.**

> The instinctive, natural way to express anger is to respond aggressively. Anger is a natural, adaptive response to threats; it inspires powerful, often aggressive, feelings and behaviors, which allow us to fight and to defend ourselves when we are attacked. A certain amount of anger, therefore, is necessary to our survival. On the other hand, we can't physically lash out at every person or object that irritates or annoys us; laws, social norms, and common sense place limits on how far our anger can take us.
>
> (APA par.5-6)

But why do we find ourselves sometimes lashing out anyway, in spite of what society says is socially acceptable? "Angry people tend to jump to- and act on- conclusions, and some of those conclusions can be very inaccurate" (APA par. 30). Once again, I have personal experience in this area. I tend to do this with my husband by prejudging what he is going to say. When he is in the middle of his explanation or reasoning, I hear a few words, sum everything up, and offer my response. When I believe his response is derogatory, I respond even faster. However, I am not always accurate with my assumptions. Basically, what this has shown me is when we have preconceived notions about what someone is going to say or about his/her motives, we tend to form conclusions rather than listening to the response in full, thinking it over, and then responding.

This is exactly what my husband always suggests that I do, and when I muster up enough patience to do it, it actually works in everyone's best interest. So, now I ask you as I had to ask myself. If you have a habit of cutting people off in the middle of their thoughts, - Do you do this to all people? If your answer is no, then ask yourself why you do it at all, or to a particular person. Is it because you believe you know exactly where they are coming from because of past experiences? Well, just as we are going through the process of changing our negative and/or detrimental behavior that took years to become embedded in us, we must be willing to believe that others can successfully go through the process of change as well. We must offer the same courtesies to them that we desire to receive while we go through our transformation.

Alternatives

There are several things that we can do instead of retaliating with verbal or physical abuse that stems from violence. After repeated attacks, our "normal" defense mechanism can become thin and our imagination can become overworked.

> It's natural to get defensive when you're criticized, but don't fight back. Instead, listen to what's underlying the words: the message that this person might feel neglected and unloved. It may take a lot of patient questioning on your part, and it may require some breathing space, but

don't let your anger—or a partner's—let a discussion spin out of control. Keeping your cool can keep the situation from becoming a disastrous one.

(APA par. 32)

I have had this to work for me. But the key is to use patience constantly and consistently.

The converse of using patience and finding out that someone's motives for saying what he/she is saying is honorable is finding out that he/she has less than positive motives for doing what he/she is doing. What do we do in this instance? The answer is still the same- Vengeance belongs to the Lord. Therefore, we must understand that revenge is never justified. "Revenge is a fighting spirit in action. It is a negative emotion, in that it sends the same hormones coursing through our body as when we feel anger. Revenge is a negative response to anger. It serves no useful purpose. Two wrongs don't make a right" (Kramer).

I know from personal experience that becoming angry and wanting revenge is natural. But once you make it a habit, it is a hard habit to break. And it may not be the case that you do it purposefully, but it becomes second nature. But in the end the result is always the same- it just isn't worth it.

Let the following poem minister to your heart. This poem was written to illustrate one of my greatest strengths that the Lord has afforded me, perseverance. By persevering through adversity, despite the mistakes that I have made, God has also afforded me an abundance of grace and mercy. Remember, you are strong and when you get weary, read Isaiah 40:31 that says, *"But they that wait upon the Lord shall renew their strength; they shall mount up with wings as eagles; they shall run, and not be weary; and they shall walk, and not faint."*

<u>Perseverance</u>

Why is it that I persevere?
Is it because I know that the end is near?
Is it because I refuse to tremble with fear?
Or, maybe because I ignore the negativity I see and hear?

Do I press toward the mark because I think I know it all?
Or is it a refusal to give up or fall?
Or because I give attention to and heed the high call?
Maybe, it's because I've found I'm strong after all.

RESENTMENT

Where Do We Go From Here?

Marching Onward

As I pondered and pondered about how to begin this chapter and as I sought the Holy Spirit's desire for this section of the book, the answer was revealed- prayer. So, in obedience let's pray.

Blessed Father,

I thank you for delivering me to the stage of the process where I can ask you where I must go from here. I continue to seek your guidance as I continue to press toward the mark of the high calling in Christ Jesus. The mark that I am striving for is freedom from the bondage of anger. I thank you Lord that the bandages are falling loose and that I can feel total victory in my grasp. I bless you now for placing a new testimony on my lips, a testimony that speaks of your healing power. Oh Jehovah Rapha, you are my healer and my strength.

Lord Father, I thank you for loving me and for covering me with your precious blood. The blood that shields my mind, guards my heart, provides temperance in my attitude, exudes patience and anoints me for service.

Lord Jesus, I thank you for the miraculous change that you are bringing about in my life. Thank you for allowing me to call you Jehovah Jirah because you have provided me with a new outlook on life and you have shown me the benefits of reshaping my perception. With your love, help and guidance, I can see my way to a brighter and more prosperous future. And for this, I thank you. In the masterless name of Jesus I pray, Amen.

Now that we have prayed and are mentally and spiritually prepared, we can move on and continue with our healing and transformation.

But first, let's review. We know how anger can manifest (which may have been a different cause for each of us) and are able to witness it in action. But now the question is- what can be done to cause the fire that burns so brightly and violently to be extinguished? The answer is plain and simple. We need to learn how to lean on our heavenly father and look to the hills from whence comes our strength. Even when we feel that we can't make it, He will be there to carry us through to our destination. It is not our own strength that we must rely upon. It would be virtually impossible to complete a transformation of this magnitude on our own human strength. This transformation can only occur in the spiritual realm.

Since this is the case, it proves that it is not flesh and blood that is our enemy, even though we are most apt to perceive it that way. Rather, as the Holy Bible tells us in Ephesians 6:12, "For we wrestle not against flesh and blood, but against principalities, against powers, against the rulers of the darkness of this world, against spiritual wickedness in high places." Therefore, because this is a spiritual issue, we must war in the spirit and not in the flesh.

Here is a set of steps that you can use to take you further in the healing process.

1.   Give the anger that you are experiencing gratitude for all the lessons that it has taught you thus far. (We should never go through a trial without learning a lesson. So imagine what is to be learned from this battle.)

- Have a session that will allow you to fully explore the anger you experience. Find a quiet place where you can be alone. Take the time to think about all what being filled with and expressing anger have taught you. As you engage in this activity, visualize your experiences in a time progression manner (chronological order). Then verbalize the experiences so that you can hear yourself speak. When you perform this activity audibly, you actually say each word and they will penetrate your psyche in a manner that would not occur if you only let the words quietly pass through your mind. Once you have reminded yourself of your anger episodes, proceed to step two.

2.   Commit to finding the positive aspects in your situation.

- Now that you have verbalized your experiences, look for the positive components in each of them. All of the lessons that you have learned may not have been pleasurable experiences and you may not find anything positive about each individual episode, but collectively you may be able to pinpoint positive factors. For example, if I look at many of the episodes that I have experienced, I may not be able to make a list of what I learned specifically from each one, but I can tell you that collectively I have learned that exercising patience and hearing someone fully verbalize his opinion will create a win-win situation for both parties engaged in the conversation.

Once discovered, accepting the positive attributes means that you have learned the lessons that God designed for you to learn. Continue to make them a part of who you are by verbally stating that you will use the lessons to become the man or woman of God that He has called you to be. Doing this will shed a positive light on the healing process that you are going through. You are not only excavating unhealthy anger from your life, but you are also receiving positive personality traits that you can feel even better about in addition.

3.   Answer the following question- What does the anger want from you?

-    Basically, that translates to- How is the Devil attempting to use this emotion against you? If you remember the Devil's purpose, that his job is to steal, kill, and destroy, then you will quickly come to the understanding that filling us with anger is yet another attempt to destroy us and strip us down to nothing.

So, what can we do to combat his attempts? Remember as mentioned earlier, you are in spiritual warfare. Consequently, you must war in the spirit. Am I suggesting that you take the Devil on? Absolutely not! The Devil is no match for you. He has much more experience with anger than you do. In order to win this battle, you must go to the Heavenly Father and consult Him and ask Him to direct your paths. The Bible tells us "the steps of a good man are ordered by the Lord" (Psalms 37:23).

4.   Now it is time to prepare for a win-win situation.

-     Decide who you want to be in the future in respect to dealing with anger and ask God to show you how to achieve it and go forth and be all that you desire to be in the name of Jesus. Write your desires down so you can reread them from time to time. They will serve as a source of encouragement and hope in a situation that seems dim.

Now that you have a plan to take you further in your journey, let me explain to you the seriousness of being an anger-filled person and the effects it can have on your body if you don't bring it under subjection. According to Dr. Brodeur, who quotes Carol Travis, "Some therapists believe that suppressed anger is the real cause of all sexual disorders, marital problems, psychosomatic illnesses, depression, suicide and all abnormal or deviant behaviors."

If you know that you already have one or more of these issues or you do not want your situation to advance and cause you to experience one of these issues, then take your life and your future by force with the power that has been afforded you through our Lord and Savior Jesus Christ. Healing is available to you, but you must do your part and the Holy Spirit will do the rest.

Here is another poem that can help you through this time of healing.

<u>Healing</u>

Today, I had a breakthrough
Demons were exercised and it was long overdue

For decades and decades, they controlled my every mood
And would not allow me to do all that I could

To see the good in people and their true worth
All I could do was protect myself from being hurt

Being defensive was my number one activity
Rather than letting people see all the good in me

I'd let my light shine and then tuck it away
To get close to me there was a price to pay

It meant showing your vulnerability without letting you see
mine
But of course that got old; it just took a long time

But now that I've made this tremendous step
I know this is something I'll never forget

Allowing myself to live a life that's true and free
Now that I've given up those old iniquities

I'm allowing God to come in and reign supreme
Because only He can manifest all my dreams

Of being open and free to the people I love

And this can only be done by casting all my cares on my master above

God has freed me and given me a chance at life
And neither my soul nor my self worth did I have to sacrifice

Thank you, Lord.

How Can I Help Someone I Love?

Walking in the Spirit

Helping or watching someone you love go through the process of being delivered from experiencing unhealthy bouts of anger is not an easy or comforting process. Many times people who are in this position do not always understand what the afflicted person is dealing with. All they see are the results of the bouts of anger. The "lack of understanding" gap causes many more misunderstandings in relationships and can cause hurts and wounds that can last a lifetime.

But with the grace of God, it does not have to be that way. To alleviate the strain of misunderstandings that can arise in relationships, I propose the following process be executed while a loved one goes through his/her process of healing. In order for this process to work, similar to the healing process, you must be willing to learn more about the person who is going through his/her deliverance, by understanding that there is much more that lies underneath the surface.

1.   To set this process in order, you must forgive the person of any hurtful words that have been uttered and/or any actions that have been performed. Without forgiveness, this entire process will fail. Remember, usually when a person acts out angrily, there is something else that is more deeply rooted that fuels his/her anger. Maybe there are patterns

that you demonstrate that cause him/her to recall the same or similar instances from his/her past. This recollection may trigger an outburst.

It is not necessarily important that you change your patterns nor am I saying that he/she should not be particularly disturbed by your behavior. It will vary from relationship to relationship as to what needs to be changed. As the two of you begin to restructure your behavior patterns, together you will learn how to navigate with one another. You will find that this process will go much smoother if you remember that you are dealing with a spirit and not the flesh and blood that is standing in front of you. So for healthy results, you must be in a positive frame of mind when dealing with spiritual matters.

2.   Patience is another virtue that plays a definite role in both processes, of healing and assisting. The area that patience is needed most is in attempting to understand a person's past and the resulting emotions. Sometimes those who witness someone going through the healing process are so anxious to be of assistance that they become overbearing with the level and/or amount of questions that they have in one sitting.

People respond differently when questioned. Some people are at the point in their healing that the retelling of their past is liberating. However, there are others who are still very much threatened by the vulnerability that exudes when they open up, but at some point in time they may open up. Then, there are others who may go through their entire healing process and never open up to the people closest to them. They sometimes opt to talk to strangers, i.e. therapists.

In many cases, this is extremely difficult for those who are outside the experience to conceptualize. But remember, people heal in their own manner. They won't necessarily go through their healing process the way you went through yours, if you have ever gone through one. It is terribly unfair to further subject them to your conditions of healing and/or understanding. Subjection to the conditions of others is most likely why individuals are filled with unhealthy anger.

3.   Create an atmosphere that is conducive for communication. Surprisingly, you will find that at times a person who is going through the healing process will want to invite you in to a safe place to discuss what he/she is feeling or experiencing internally.

Waiting for an invitation may be a little tough to conceptualize because of the closeness that you share. The closeness that you share may lead you to believe that you have an automatic entrance into every part of someone else's life, but that simply is not true.

Look at it this way. Sometimes it takes decades for someone to address his/her issue. He/she may have locked the door to that particular issue and have not fully explored the issue's effects him/herself, so letting you in to try to figure it out for him/her is virtually impossible. Again patience is key, but create the environment so when the person is ready, he/she can come to you.

4.   Express your concern, love, and understanding. Concern and love are not usually hard to demonstrate. Understanding, on the other hand, may be extremely hard to demonstrate especially if you really don't understand or simply can't relate to what someone else is going through. A lack of understanding can lead to

judgments being passed, hurtful words spoken, or unnecessary actions being taken.

This is where prayer comes in. James 1:5 says, *"If any of you lack wisdom, let him ask of God, that giveth to all men liberally, and upbraideth not; and it shall be given him."*

5.   Verbally embrace your loved one with encouraging words that tell him/her the wonderful changes you have noticed in his/her personality. When offering words of encouragement be forewarned to only give praise when praise is due, not when you want to illicit a change. When a person is in a process of change, he/she knows when changes have been made. He/she will appreciate you noticing too but may not appreciate unwarranted flattery because it is a struggle to change and when change occurs it is appreciated by all and should not be taken lightly.

With these five steps, you can make the road to recovery for your loved one a smooth trip. He/she will embrace you and cherish your support always.

Demonic Forces

The Evil behind the Attitude

When confronted with emotions such as uncontrollable anger, it is always best to determine how the emotion evolved. In my situation, as disclosed earlier, the anger I experienced was due to the molestation/rape that I experienced as a child and teenager. Of course, there were probably other situations in my life that could have fueled the anger, but primarily I believe that my bouts of anger were due to the incidents of molestation/rape that left me feeling betrayed and alone.

However, I later came to learn that I was not the only one in my family that experienced molestation or other types of sexual abuse. In learning this, I discovered that my family had been afflicted by a generational curse that had traveled down through generations and had even passed to the generation after me. Basically, that means that possibly a demonic spirit of molestation and/or rape was assigned to my family and unless the curse was broken, it would continue to travel from generation to generation.

Upon learning this, I began to read the book *Curses* by Dick Bernal. In this book, Bernal discusses how generational curses operate and what must be done to break them. This book lent to a better understanding of the causes and effects of generational curses.

Also, I read Dr. Rebecca Brown's book titled *Unbroken Curses*. Dr. Brown's book, like *Curses,* also discusses generational curses and the procedures for both exposing them and eradicating them.

Another book that I found extremely interesting was *Pigs in the Parlor* by Frank and Ida Mae Hammond, which was referred to me by a sister in Christ. Although this book did not focus on generational curses specifically, it did discuss how a person can open the door to demons and what must be done in order for them to be expurgated.

There are several resources that may be available to you in your local Bible bookstore that you may find helpful in understanding how demonic spirits work. Also, it is always a good idea to speak to the individual who serves as your spiritual covering about your situation. He/she may be able to provide spiritual guidance about your situation.

Reaching a Milestone

A Fresh Anointing

I pray that at this point in the book and in your life that you feel the way that I do about what you have learned and experienced in regards to being free from anger. Personally, I feel like a new person. I feel a sense of calm in my spirit. I feel liberated and renewed. I know that it was my choice to either continue to be a victim or I can move into the position of victor. How about you?

Are you going to choose life as a victor and live as a true example of a son or daughter of the Most High God, or are you going to die a slow death as you live as a perpetual victim? The Holy Bible discusses the choice between life and death in Deuteronomy 30:19. And it clearly states that we should choose life. God's Word is given to us freely and we have the choice to live our lives in any manner that we choose.

However, if we desire to have the fulfilled life that our heavenly father promises us we can have, then we will follow His commandments because that is the only way that the life that we desire can manifest. That means that we will choose life.

What that means in our discussion of anger is letting go of the demons that have plagued our lives by giving them a one-way ticket back to hell.

Now that the Lord has taken me to another level by allowing me to experience His miraculous healing power in the area of anger, I feel confident to pray for your healing in this area as well.

Precious Lord,

You are an awesome God, who never ceases to amaze me. Your generosity, grace, kindness, and love mean so much to me. And Father, I know that in you there is no respect of persons; you do not favor one of us over the other. So Father, it is my prayer that you will do for the readers of this book what you have done for me. They desire freedom, just as I did.

I intercede now, Father, on their behalf. I enter the throne room of grace in search for a cure of the madness that encapsulates them. The madness that works as grief and bitterness causes evil to exude from the inner most part of them. We desire, instead, for the purity of love to replace the bitterness and hatred oh Father, in the name of Jesus. Lord, we want to be more like you. We want your ways to be our ways.

So, we are willing to step up and out and be transparent. We are willing to step out of our comfort zone and into the unknown because we trust that you are there and we seek your face and your loving arms. Encapsulate them oh Lord with your loving arms just as you do for me. Oh Lord, I thank because I can feel you moving on their behalf. I thank you for being a God of your word, a God who can move mountains and cross oceans to see about our needs, for you are the great I Am.

Oh, we love you Lord. And we thank you for your supernatural power that meets all our needs, in this instance and all others. For you are Jehovah Rapha, Jehovah Nissi, Jehovah Shalom, El Shaddai, Prince of

Peace, King of Kings, Lord of Lords, the Alpha and the Omega. I enter this prayer in the name of the Son of Man, the Son of God, Jesus Christ.
Amen.

BROKENNESS

PART
TWO

AND THEN HELL REALLY BROKE LOOSE!

What an Epiphany!

What a Revelation!

Just when I thought I had it all figured out and I was feeling great about the difference the writing of this book has made in my life and I had experienced an emotional lift of the anger, the Holy Spirit spoke to me and said, "Daughter, don't be fooled. The battle that you are fighting today is not yours. And the enemy has been very crafty in leading you to believe that you have not forgiven your trespassers when you have. He is leading you to believe that all the anger that you have bottled up inside of you is from your past when in reality it is from your present." At that point, the cycle seemed to start all over again and I became very discouraged and did not know how I was going to see my healing come to manifestation. I stopped writing the book and wanted to trash it. The enemy almost convinced me to believe that my transformation was not to be a reality. However, on a positive note, I was halfway there because I was freed from committing horrendous acts of violence. I do still have verbal outbursts and want to throw objects across the room, but using balled fists like in a boxing match has ceased.

Sure, my past was a catalyst for my present behaviors, but I always had a feeling that the rage that I was experiencing was more than just unresolved issues of my past. I remember going through my stage of extending forgiveness to my trespassers because I did not desire to have unforgiveness blocking my blessings. However, the enemy had led me to believe that all my past emotions were not in the past but were still very much alive in me. But I soon had to stop and realize that that was just another crafty trick of the enemy.

As I began to examine my present life conditions, I noticed that changes had taken place that I was pleased with while others I was most displeased. I had recently entered into marriage with my second husband after being divorced for nine years. Entering into this relationship with me were my children from my previous marriage, who at the time were fourteen and eleven years of age.

My new husband and I were married after a unique sort of relationship. We met at our church of two locations (east and west locations) where each of us was a member of the opposite location; I attended the east location and he attended the west location. After meeting, we became friends who spoke sometimes for days on end (in the beginning) and from there only maybe twice a month. In a year's time, in the midst of the conversations, we only had outings a total of four times, having dinner or lunch.

Finally, ten months later my soon-to-be husband approached me one Saturday afternoon and asked me a question that simply knocked me off my feet. He asked me if I loved him. This caught me by total surprise because we had never discussed love nor had we discussed us as a couple. We knew that there was an attraction between the two of us but we never directly addressed it. In response to his question I said, "No. I don't, but that doesn't mean that I don't believe I never will. I just have never entertained the idea because so much seems to get in the way of positive communication." By this I meant that we didn't seem to get along well for weeks at a time. It always seemed like we needed to take a break and then begin speaking again. As a result of our previous interaction, I had entertained the thought of us getting together but would always reject it.

Obviously that idea of rejecting us as a couple did not remain with me because two nights after I answered his question, I had a talk with my heavenly father and consulted His take on the situation. After that, I put all my inhibitions aside and decided to open my heart and found myself falling deeply in love with the man I considered to be the man of my dreams. We were married four months later.

Those feelings of love were soon coupled by feelings of confusion caused by behavior patterns that demonstrated a variety of emotions on the part of my husband, not to mention any thought patterns that I had that needed to be transformed. I guess our union, although it obtained many recipes for success, obtained a recipe for disaster because of the baggage we both brought to the relationship. Although we had both forgiven those that had trespassed against us throughout various eras of our lives, we both still needed to go through our healing processes.

To make a long story short, in moments of intense frustration and anger I committed many acts against my husband in an effort to defend myself, rather than turn the situation over to God. However, as stated earlier in the book, regardless of the behavior of others we cannot allow their insecurities or their sinful behavior to encourage us to react in a violent manner. However, I found myself doing it time and time again, even when I felt bad afterwards. And it is not to say that I was the perfect wife and that all our marital problems stemmed from him because that is far from the truth. The point I'm trying to emphasize is we can always find and make excuses for our behavior. But the reality is there is no excuse for acting un-Godly in our actions or words.

What often prevented me from reacting in a violent manner was reading and rereading Part One of this book along with the scriptures that are quoted within, listening to sermons, and reading spiritual books on violence. However, the primary reason I found to change my behavior was to realize what the enemy had planned for my life, which was in direct contradiction for what God had designed for me.

Neither my husband nor I could wait for the other to be healed before we decided to get our act together. Operating in an unhealed condition always gives a person a reason to act out and/or utter unfounded comments. I had to decide that I would not be trapped in a world of confusion and that I would just stay focused on the Lord and His design for my life and I knew that self-destruction guided by the enemy was not the key.

The enemy wanted my husband and I to believe that we were each others worst enemy, and we bought into his tricks time and time again. At some point, we needed to stop fighting each other and join camps and fight against the enemy. As the word asks in Deuteronomy 32: 30, *"How can one chase a thousand and two put ten thousand to flight?"* Therefore, we could have fought many of the demons from our relationship, but constantly being worn and feeling defeated our relationship endured many challenges. So, I guess anyone can see who held the lead in that battle. But nevertheless, we constantly decided that we would not be defeated and that we would put our trust in God. Rather, we would stand and fight the good fight of faith.

Rising Above Your Emotions

Stand Firm

The morning after writing the previous chapter, I turned on TBN as I was preparing for work. After the conclusion of Joyce Meyer's broadcast, Dr. Creflo Dollar appeared on the screen. His sermon for the day was titled "Rising above Your Emotions," after which this chapter is titled. I did not have an opportunity to watch the entire broadcast, but I was able to hear just what the Lord wanted me to hear.

Unbeknownst to me, the purpose of my watching the broadcast was for God to have an opportunity to confirm the word that He had given me the night before. Dr. Dollar stated, "Your emotions will tell you something different every time, but the Word of God will remain the same." What Dr. Dollar meant by this was that in a given situation our emotions may tell us to react in a different way each time we experience that same situation. But if we follow the Word of God, we will get the same response each time. Therefore, we must stand on the Word of God and follow His commandments. We cannot be led by our flesh (from which our emotions stem) because it may mislead us.

Dr. Dollar illustrated his point by using the words of our Lord and Savior as he prepared to take the cross. As stated in the book of Matthew, in 26:39, *"Going a little farther, he fell with his face to the ground and prayed, 'My Father, if it is possible, may this cup be taken from me'."* This request was made from his human condition, from his flesh, because He was weighted down from the sins of this world. But as we know, Jesus was on earth to fulfill a destiny, as we all are, and he continued by saying, *"Yet not as I will, but as you will."* So, in the end He stayed with the Word of God.

This illustration demonstrates how our emotions easily play a part in our decision making. It is as though it is human nature. But our emotions and logic do not play an integral part in our faith walk. Remember faith is the substance of things hoped for; the evidence of things unseen. That means we should always let the Word of God be our guide. If we fail to do this, we will find ourselves constantly faced with battles. The only way to overcome the battles is to follow the instructions of the Lord.

Proverbs 3: 5-6 says, *"Trust in the LORD with all thine heart; and lean not unto thine own understanding. In all thy ways acknowledge him, and he shall direct thy paths."* If we allow God to be the pilot and navigator of our lives, we can never go wrong. But in order to do this we have to mature spiritually. We can know God's Word and deliver God's Word, but until we live God's Word and give Him the reigns of our lives, we will never be truly free from the bondage that encapsulates us. Getting to this point in our spiritual walk happens individually. No one can take us there, but it is our willingness to be obedient and live a God-inspired life that will allow us to reach this point.

The Reformation

Making Noticeable Progress

How can you tell if you are being transformed from an anger-filled condition? How can you tell that you simply haven't been on your best behavior and that your temper isn't simply lying dormant waiting for the next victim? Often times those who are anger-filled don't explode on a daily basis or in a multitude of situations. Rather, only specific types of situations or interacting with specific people will cause them to have outbursts. I found this to be true for me. Therefore, to truly know if you are being transformed from an anger-filled person to a person that can control his/her temper, it may be necessary for you to be placed into the situation that causes you to experience unhealthy anger. Because if you are not tested and tried, how do you know that you have passed the test? (This may not be true for all people. Be very careful and let God guide you in this area.)

For me, I noticed that in many instances I was being purposefully provoked. After several incidents of being provoked, I could see how I really needed to control my emotions and temper and not allow others to further antagonize me to act out or retaliate. We must decide that we are in control of our emotions and that God has given us power to overcome them even when others seem to want to keep us bound by provoking us in an effort to see if we will respond as usual, rather than helping free us by being nurturing. After having contemplated this for a couple of weeks, once after being provoked I thought about changing my behavior and not using their behavior as an excuse for my actions; I simply walked away and had a seat. This act was very liberating and marked a change in my behavior from that point forward.

What was also inspirational was that I wasn't the one who noticed a change in my behavior. It was a friend that I had shared these incidents with that pointed out the change in my behavior. So at this point in the writing of the book, I celebrate the progress in my transformation and I count the days of less amounts of anger exuding from me, even when I seemingly have more reasons to actually be angry.

I encourage you to do the same. Take note of changes in your behavior. It doesn't mean that you won't have a set back or relapse. If you do, just don't be too hard on yourself. Change, although natural, can be difficult, especially when behavior patterns have been formed. Instead, keep pressing toward the mark as it says in Philippians 3:14, *"I press toward the mark for the prize of the high calling of God in Christ Jesus."* Let God define what the mark is for you and work toward His desired end, if you can align your will with His. As Jesus says in John 3:38, *"For I came down from heaven, not to do mine own will, but the will of him that sent me."* We must always be willing to do God's will and not our own. Giving in to our will, which is directed by our flesh, is what has caused us to be in the situation that we are in now. So, as part of our reformation we must *"not be conformed to the this world: but be transformed by the renewing of your mind, that ye may prove what is that good, and acceptable, and perfect, will of God"* (Romans 12:2). And if we practice patience, and wait upon the Lord, He shall renew our strength (Isaiah 40:31). This will enable us to walk as God has called us to walk and not in the detrimental way that we have become accustomed to.

x

Final Word

Know Your Target

Part Two of this book focused on the realization of my current possession of anger which stemmed from issues of my past but was a reality of my "right now" situation. Part One and Part Two together were designed to lead you to successfully addressing your issues of anger. Although you may know where the anger stems from, you must look seriously at other factors that may secretly creep in to cause further confusion and throw you off focus while in your healing process. Be constantly aware of who you are dealing with- Satan- The Trickster, who comes to steal, kill, and destroy. Remember, the Word says, *"We are not ignorant of Satan's devices"* (2 Cor. 2:11). So always watch and pray and remain clad with the full armour of God (Ephesians 6:11) and allow the Holy Spirit to minister to you and guide you as you go through your healing process.

I encourage you to really be sure of the source from where your anger emanates and not be led by your emotions. If you confront the wrong issue, you will not be working efficiently to eradicate the problem. Therefore, rather than trusting your emotions to tell you what your problem is, listen to the Holy Spirit. Let Him be your guide. Jeremiah 10: 23 says, *"O Lord, I know that the way of man is not in himself: it is not a man that walketh to direct his steps."* So who does direct his steps? The Bible tells us in Psalms 37:23 that the steps of a good man are ordered by Lord. So, as a good, holy, and acceptable servant of the Most High

God, let Him order your steps today and lead you to the right path.

I leave you with this prayer as I can now stand before God and declare that the bondage has been loosed and God's Word has been bound to my situation.

Oh merciful and forgiving God,
We come in all sincerity in the spirit of repentance of all ungodly acts and thanking you for delivering us from our anger-filed conditions. Father God, for those who are still works in progress we pray that they too be loosed from bondage and that they daily apply your word to their lives. We profess freedom for every person who experiences unhealthy anger and we declare their speedy deliverance in the name of Jesus.

Father God, we pray that we continue to press toward the mark of the high calling in Christ Jesus. We declare that we are not victims but victors because as a royal priesthood we are conquerors and shall not be defeated. We will stand righteous as we are protected by the impenetrable blood of the lamb.

Oh Father, as we cry out unto your name we thank you for being a sovereign god, a loving god, a merciful god, and a gracious god. We thank you for being the Alpha and the Omega. We thank you for loving us when we didn't love ourselves. We thank you for looking past our faults and seeing our needs. We thank you for your healing virtue. We thank you for your cleansing power as you continue to cleanse us from all unrighteousness.

Oh, we greatly esteem your name because you are worthy of all the praise. We praise you for your love; we praise you for your direction; we praise you for all you have done, all you are doing, and all you will do. We praise you because even though we have all fallen and come short, you are there to pick up the pieces and restore us. Thank you for restoration Father. Thank you for replenishing us. Thank you for keeping us in the shadows. Thank you, Lord for removing bitterness, hatred, envy, strife, jealousy, and contention. Thank you for restoring us to our rightful positions in you.

We thank you, we love you, and we adore you. In Jesus' name, Amen.

In the name of our savior, Jesus Christ, with uplifted heads, march on soldiers. March on. Victory is yours.

UNFORGIVENESS

After Word

At the completion of this project, I am very elated with the success it has brought to my life and the level of peace and calmness that has become a part of my daily being. I am also definitely excited about the success and triumph that it will bring to the lives of others. It is my prayer that they will also experience pleasurable auras of peace and triumph in the midst of the storms of life.

If you are reading this After Word, then more than likely you have finished reading the book. If you have noticed progress in your healing then you have just cause to celebrate. No victory is too small. Stop right now and do a dance all over Satan's head and proclaim total victory and know that God will continue to work in your life.

Remember, each day presents a new challenge. But you can overcome them all. As the Bible says, "Many are the afflictions of the righteous: but the LORD delivereth him out of them all" (Psalms 34:19). So, as we have proclaimed victory to be ours throughout the entire book don't stop now. Satan is waiting to sneak back in and steal your joy. Fill the places where anger used to reside with love, joy, peace, longsuffering, kindness, goodness, faithfulness, gentleness, and self-control. These are the fruits of the spirit and they will sustain you. Be forever blessed as you walk in His peace.

References

American Psychological Association (APA). (2005).
Controlling Anger – Before It Controls You.
Washington, DC. www.apa.org/pubinfo/anger.html

Bernal, Dick. *Curses.*

Brown, Rebecca, Dr. *Unbroken Curses.*

Hammond, Frank and Ida Mae. (1973, 2004). *Pigs in the Parlor.* Impact Christian Books. Kirkwood, MO.

Kramer, Susan. (1998). Anger Analyzed from a spiritual point of view. Santa Barbara, CA USA.

Unleashed Anger, Anger Unleashed Workbook

Chapter One
Times of Innocence

Everyone's issue of anger begins somewhere. My roots of anger formed from the molestation and rape that I suffered as a small child and teenager.

1. Identify the source(s) of your anger.

_____

_____

_____

_____

_____

_____

_____

_____

_____

_____

2. Write a brief summary of each event.

_____

_____

_____

_____

_____

_____

_____

_____

3. How does recalling the event make you feel?

_____

_____

_____

_____

_____

_____

_____

_____

4. Outside of doing this assignment, how often do you recall these events? What triggers the recollection of these events?

_____

_____

_____

_____

_____

_____

_____

_____

NOTES

Chapter Two
Warning Signs
Bouts of Anger

In the book, I shared several incidents where I displayed violence. List the episodes and a brief description of each that you experienced due to your affliction of anger. Be prepared to share these with the class/group if you feel comfortable.

You may want to write about incidents that cover a specific time period, ie the last five years. This time frame should be relative to the amount of years that your condition was really noticeable.

_____

_____

_____

_____

_____

_____

_____

_____

_____

_____

_____

_____

_____

_____

_____

_____

_____

NOTES

Chapter Three

Self-Reflection

A Look in the Mirror

Doing a self examination is healthy, if and only if we are willing to be painfully honest with ourselves. In doing a self examination, it is always important to have a specific focus of what characteristics or qualities to search one's self for.

In the self examination that you should conduct in an effort to be healed from an anger-filled condition, make a list of both positive and negative personality traits that you believe you possess. Do not focus on what others have said, for this is a self reflection not a people pole.

Positive Traits

_____

_____

_____

_____

_____

_____

Negative Traits

_____

_____

_____

_____

_____

_____

_____

_____

_____

Chapter Four
Feeling Provoked
Don't Give In

As we go through our process of being healed from our anger-filled conditions, we may become painfully aware of those things/people that so easily beset us.

For this activity, make a list of things/people/incidents/behaviors that easily provoke you to react in an unhealthy manner, even if the situation no longer exists in your life.

1. _____

_____

_____

2. _____

_____

_____

3. _____

_____

_____

NOTES

Chapter Five
Where Do We Go From Here?
Marching Onward

Have you ever heard the phrase, "If you fail to plan, you plan to fail"? That phrase is applicable to your deliverance as well.

At this point, you have admitted your affliction and you have expressed your desire to be free. After reading the chapter, what do you feel is best for the next several steps in your healing process and why? Remember, each person goes through his/her healing process individually, as directed by the Holy Spirit; therefore, your process may be different from someone else's.

List your projected steps here.

1. _____

_____

2. _____

_____

3. _____

_____

4. _____

_____

5. _____

_____

6. _____

_____

7. _____

_____

8. _____

_____

9. _____

_____

If the steps have not yet been revealed to you, skip this chapter and complete it when you are able.

Chapter Six

Demonic Forces
The Evil behind the Attitude

This chapter discusses several books that lent to my understanding of demonic forces and the power they have as afforded to them by Satan. However, these same books elaborately discussed the power believers have in the name of Jesus, which is above all other names including Satan's.

For this lesson, visit your local book store or library (or even visit the world wide web) and choose a source that explains how believers can be over comers. Be prepared to discuss the text you chose in class. Bring the text with you.

NOTES

Chapter Seven

Reaching a Milestone
A Fresh Anointing

At various points during the healing process, milestones (points of victory) are reached. Review your situation, and write a letter to God explaining what He has done for you thus far and thank God for all He has done to turn the situation around in your life.

_____

_____

_____

_____

_____

_____

_____

_____

_____

_____

_____

NOTES

Chapter Eight
What an Epiphany!
What a Revelation!

As we go through our journey of being healed, we must be cognizant of the roots of our anger and any resulting branches.

Since you began your healing process, have you had any revelations about other issues that cause you to be angry in addition to the initial incidents that you experienced that helped to form the roots?

Describe the incidents below.

_____

_____

_____

_____

_____

_____

_____

_____

Chapter Nine
Rising Above Your Emotions
Stand Firm

Each of us has acted out of our emotions at some time in our life. For many of us, that some time has actually been many times. However, if we are honest, we will admit that acting out may not have been the wisest thing to do.

Choose one situation where you acted/responded from your anger. Also, discuss what would have been a better plan for dealing with the situation. How does reflection help you to determine future behaviors?

_____

_____

_____

_____

_____

_____

_____

Chapter Ten

A Final Word

Encourage others in the class. Tell them of any progress that you may have noticed. Remember though, in a classroom/group setting you may not experience people in an anger-filled condition. Therefore, there may not be noticeable changes in that respect. However, you may notice changes in temperament, tone of voice, body language, etc. Share your perceptions with members of your class/group.

Prayers

(for the success of this project and the complete healing and deliverance of the author and her readers)

Cassundra,
This is my prayer.

Father God,
Thank you for my daughter Cassundra. I know she is your child, but you entrusted her to me.

Thank you for guiding, blessing, leading, and protecting her life.

Father God, thank you for giving her the wisdom to understand and overcome anger in her life and the willingness to write this book to enable others to take control of life's anger and not let life take control of them.

Father, bless this book, and let it be a blessing to others who read it and also a blessing for new beginnings for Cassundra.

In Jesus' name,
Amen

Your mother,
Gloria L. Harrison

Father, I honor your Name.

There is no other name under heaven that is greater than yours. I bow my knees humbly before you making my request to you and thanking you in advance for all things that you have done and will do. Lord, I ask you in the Name of Jesus that you will heal -according to your Word- and bring complete healing to many that are victims to the uncontrollable violent of anger. For it is by your stripes and the power of the Holy Ghost that you have given us the power to be completely free. Lord, I thank you that you have allowed me to be angry according to your Word (Eph. 4:26), but not to the degree that it causes me to sin against you. I'm thanking you in advance for each day that is declared to be a victorious day of joy in the soul and peace in the mind and heart. Each day I will say, that I Am Free and declare that I am no longer in bondage because the Lord has freed me.

This I pray in Jesus' divine name Amen.

Your friend,
Evangelist Mary Jackson

Father, in the name of Jesus, I thank you for being who you are: the God that boldly declares, "I am that I am." I praise you for being my healer, deliver, baptizer, peace, righteousness, provider, victory, and joy. You are my all in all, and I thank you for being the captain of my soul. You are the One who orders and directs my footsteps, activities, actions, deeds and thoughts.

Because of my knowledge of your will for my life, I can now release and cast all my cares, fears, frustrations, disappointments, angers, aughts, and woes unto you for you care for me.

Father, I will no longer hold anger in my heart for it births works of evil. I will not lash out but I will learn techniques on how to turn the other cheek, to study, to be quiet and to bridle my tongue, for it is the most unruly part of my body, and I will seek to receive sound counsel according to your word.

I thank you for declaring your works from the beginning and loving me with an everlasting love that could only come from you.

I ask and receive forgiveness for my sins and declare that I have been cleansed through the washing of the Word of God.

I seal this prayer with the precious blood of Jesus.
Amen.

Your Friend,
Evangelist Marcella Flanangan

Father, I thank you that each person who reads this book becomes healed in some way whether emotionally, verbally, sexually or physically.

Father, I thank you for the author of this book. She has shared her pain and suffering with the world. I thank you Father, God that she has allowed you to remove the character flaws that have held her in bondage for many years. Father, you have rescued her from the dominion of darkness and brought her to the light. Thank you, Lord, for she now walks as a child of light. The abuse is exposed and reproved by the light. It is made visible and clear because where everything is visible and clear there is light. Thank you, Father that the author had the wisdom and knowledge to lean not on her own understanding, but to lean on you. Your Word tells us when we've done all "Stand."

Father, in the mighty name of Jesus, I speak prosperity in the life of the author. May her life be filled with richness as her book goes forth changing the lives of everyone who read it.

Father, I pray that the author and her readers live their lives to the fullest and they will know that when it hurts to look back but they are scared to look ahead, they will just look beside them and their best friend will be there as a guide. He's closer than a brother.

Thanks you, Father for all that you are going to do in the lives of many. I pray that they put on the whole armor of God and the shield of faith protects them from all the fiery darts of the wicked.

In the mighty name of Jesus. Amen.

Your aunt,
Julia Lary

Set Free

Included Inside

UNLEASHED ANGER, ANGER UNLEASHED

Dr. C. White-Elliott

Set Free is a work of non-fiction; however, names have been excluded or changed to protect all involved parties.

All scripture are from the King James Version of the Holy Bible, unless otherwise noted.

CLF Publishing, LLC.
9161 Sierra Ave, Ste. 203C
Fontana, CA 92335
www.clfpublishing.org

Cover design by Senir Design. Contact information- info@senirdesign.com.

ISBN # 978-0-9961971-4-4

Printed in the United States of America.

Dedication

I dedicate this book to all my readers who find comfort in the
words that flow across the pages.

God is an awesome god, who is the author and finisher of our faith
(Hebrews 12:2). He knows our expected end (Jeremiah 29:11).

Trust Him to order your steps and direct your paths (Psalm 37:23).
He will not fail you!

Acknowledgements

I acknowledge the Triune God: God, the Father; God, the Son; and God, the Holy Spirit for the guidance that was bestowed upon me during the writing of this book. Thank you for bringing back incidences to my memory, to demonstrate to my readers and to me how truly an awesome god you are to have moved in my life the way you have and the way you do.

Father, my life is in your hands,
today, tomorrow and forever more.

Table of Contents

Introduction

Ten years ago in 2005, I wrote *Unleashed Anger, Anger Unleashed,* the book that I pray you read before starting *Set Free*. If for some reason you did not read *Unleashed Anger, Anger Unleashed* and you jumped over to *Set Free*, I recommend you go back and read it, so the information included within *Set Free* will make sense because the books are sequential.

Ten years ago, I came to terms with my anger issues. I always understood that I could be volatile; however, I thought I could control my temper - until specific incidents show me otherwise. My awakening occurred as I became increasingly knowledgeable about the spirit world. Consequently, I began to understand that I had the unclean spirits of uncontrollable anger and bouts of rage. I then had to make a decision about whether I wanted to remain in my current condition and grow increasingly worse as I had over the last twenty-five years, or if I wanted to be clean and walk completely in the spirit of our Lord and Savior Jesus Christ and not in my flesh. As stated in at least *Unleashed Anger, Anger Unleashed,* I chose to be free in the name of Jesus.

Now ten years later, I am able to look back over the last decade and declare that I have been *set free* in the name of Jesus. Between the time I wrote *Unleashed Anger, Anger Unleashed* to the writing of this book, several incidents occurred, and each one demonstrated to me where I stood with the spirit of anger. Those incidents let me know whether anger was still part of my persona or if I were indeed free. I am pleased to announce that I am free from uncontrollable anger and bouts of rage!

Do I ever experience anger? Of course, I do. Anger is a natural emotion that is part of the human make up. This is evident in the Bible because it tells us to be angry and sin not (Ephesians 4:26). Being angry in and of itself is not a problem. How we choose to deal with our anger, however, can be problematic.

The purpose of *Set free* is to encourage someone who may be dealing with an unclean spirits. Whether it has been one year, ten years, or twenty years, you can have the spirit released from you, and you can walk in complete freedom. Satan only has the control that we give him, but we must know and understand that Jesus has given us power, and it is our right to exercise that power to the fullest extent. We, as the people of God, will not and should not take a backseat to the enemy to be his puppet and to do his bidding. Personally, I have chosen to stand up and declare the works of the Lord and to no longer be used by the enemy!

This book will include a discussion and clarification of exactly what unclean spirits are, the deliverance process, what to do after you have been delivered from an unclean spirit, how to know you have actually been delivered, and how to stay delivered.

Enjoy your reading!

Chapter One
Unclean Spirits

Let's begin our discussion with the Word of God. Galatians 5:16-24 states, "This *I say then, Walk in the Spirit, and ye shall not fulfil the lust of the flesh. For the flesh lusteth against the Spirit, and the Spirit against the flesh: and these are contrary the one to the other: so that ye cannot do the things that ye would. But if ye be led of the Spirit, ye are not under the law. Now the works of the flesh are manifest, which are* these; *Adultery, fornication, uncleanness, lasciviousness, Idolatry, witchcraft, hatred, variance, emulations, wrath, strife, seditions, heresies, Envyings, murders, drunkenness, revellings, and such like: of the which I tell you before, as I have also told you in time past, that they which do such things shall not inherit the kingdom of God. But the fruit of the Spirit is love, joy, peace, longsuffering, gentleness, goodness, faith, Meekness, temperance: against such there is no law. And they that are Christ's have crucified the flesh with the affections and lusts."*

If a person exhibits any of the works of the flesh (negative behavior patterns) that are listed above, it is a definite sign that healing is needed in order to be set free from ungodly spirits. Once a person is free from ungodly spirits, in turn, he/she can take on the fruit of the spirit as mentioned above.

Being set free from ungodly spirits is a desire for many, both believers and non-believers alike. However, it has been said believers cannot be "possessed" by the devil. That statement, to a certain degree, is true. However, to promote clarity and understanding, the statement warrants an explanation. What that declaration means is believers cannot be *fully* controlled by the enemy. Demons cannot "possess" a believer, in the respect of complete and full possession. For, possession implies ownership, and believers have already been bought with a price. We belong to the Lord Jesus Christ because He bought us with His shed blood on Calvary's cross. However, that does not mean that we won't, because we often do, unknowingly give control of areas of our life to demons (unclean spirits) by the choices we make. Therefore, they can "possess" *areas* of our life.

Dr. Charles Stanley says, "A Christian cannot be totally possessed by demons. However, invasion into the life of a believer is certainly possible and probably more common than we will ever know. Consequently, believers can take on mannerisms and behaviors that are not Christ-like."

How is this possible you ask? There are several contributing factors. First, we (humans) are comprised of three components: spirit, soul, and body. We are spirits that have a soul and are housed in a body. When we accept Christ as our personal savior, the Holy Spirit dwells within our spirit, not our flesh and not our soul. The body (the flesh) constantly wars against our spirit. Our spirit wants to please God, but our soul (mind and emotions) and flesh want to please themselves (Matthew 26:41). When we opt to gratify the flesh and the soul, these are the areas the evil spirits dwell in.

Second, Satan is the prince and the power of the air (Ephesians 2:2). He was given a measure of power in this earth realm when Adam and Eve willfully sinned in the garden. He knows what our weaknesses are, and he loves to tempt us. Does he, therefore, trap us into doing his evil biddings? Of course not. I Corinthians 10:13 says, *"There hath no temptation taken you but such as is common to man: but God is faithful, who will not suffer you to be tempted above that ye are able; but will with the temptation also make a way to escape, that ye may be able to bear it."* We are not forced by Satan to submit to sinful acts. We *choose* to indulge in the sinful temptations that taunt us. But, every action has a reaction. When we choose to indulge in temptations that are placed before us and are sinful, we open the door for unclean spirits to enter in.

Third, we can open doors to unclean spirits by harboring unforgiveness in our heart (usually due to something that happened earlier in our life, such as abuse in childhood, bruising, and/or rejection), or by being involved with witchcraft, such as horoscopes, astrology, tarot cards, fortune telling, or Ouija boards. To determine whether or not an unclean spirit resides in your temple, continue reading.

The characteristics listed in the two lists on the next several pages merit a closer look when they are *pronounced, persistent or recurrent* over a period of time, or *progressive* - tending to become more, rather than less, extreme. When someone possesses one or more of the behaviors from either list, he/she may be calling out for help, demonstrating signs that deliverance is needed.

1. **Confused or disordered thinking:** loss of touch with reality - delusions (persistence of erroneous convictions in the face of contrary evidence) - hallucinations; disconnected speech.

2. **Obsessions:** absorption with a subject or idea to the exclusion of others - compulsions - uncontrollable urges.

3. **Inability to cope:** with minor problems - with daily routine.

4. **Difficulty in making and/or keeping friends:** poor social skills - isolation, withdrawal from society - loner lifestyle.

5. **A pattern of failure across the board:** at school - at work - in sports - in personal relationships.

6. **Prolonged or severe depression:** suicide threats and/or attempts.

7. **Immaturity:** infantile behavior (such as bed-wetting) - over dependence on the mother (excessive clinging as a child and continuing dependence in teens and twenties) - failure to keep pace with peer group.

8. **A series of physical ailments,** which do not run a typical course and/or fail to respond to treatment.

9. **Neglect of personal hygiene** (disheveled and unsanitary surroundings) or exaggerated concern for order and for cleanliness.

10. **Difficulty adjusting** to new people and places.

11. **Undue anxiety and worry:** phobias - feelings of being persecuted.

12. **Too much or too little sleep**.

13. **Excessive self-centeredness:** indifference to other people's feelings, doings, ideas - lack of sympathy with another's pain or need.

14. **Substantial rapid weight** - gain or loss.

15. **Muted, flat emotions** (absence of angry / delighted / sorrowing reactions to stimuli) or inappropriate emotions (sharp, inexplicable mood swings - silliness at serious moments, unpredictable tears).

16. **Negative self-image and outlook:** inferiority complex - feelings of worthlessness.

17. **Frequent random changes of plans:** inability to stick with a job, a school program, a living arrangement - failure to keep appointments, abide by decisions.

18. **Extreme aggressiveness** (combativeness, hostility, violence, rage) or exaggerated docility (lack of normal competitiveness and self-assertion - refusal to confront, avoidance of argument).

19. **Risk-taking**: taking unsafe risks.

20. **Lack of zest and enthusiasm:** listlessness, sadness, mood habitually down - limited or missing sense of humor.

In addition to the characteristics listed on the previous page, below is a list of spirits believers can possess. Read the list carefully to see if any resonate with you.

Spirit of anger (bouts of rage) (Eph. 4:26)
Spirit of infirmity or weakness (Luke 13:11)
Spirit of antichrist (I John 4:3)
Spirit of fear (II Tim. 1:7)
Deaf spirit (Mark 9:25)
Perverse spirit (Isa. 19:14)
Dumb spirit (Mark 9:25)
Sorrowful spirit (I Sam. 1:15)

Blind spirit (Matt. 9:27)

Spirit of slumber (Rom. 11:8)

Foul spirit (Mark 9:25; Rev. 18:2)

Spirit of whoredoms (Hos. 5:4)

Unclean spirit (Matt. 14:43; Mark 1:23, 26; 3:30; 5:2,8, 7:25)

Destroying spirit (Deut. 13:15)

Evil spirit (Judges 9:23; I Sam. 16:14-16, 23; 18:10; 19:9)

Spirit of divination (Acts 16:16)

Another spirit (II Cor. 11:4)

Spirit of bondage (Rom. 8:15)

Hasty of spirit (Prov. 14:29)

Spirit of error (I John 4:6)

Haughty spirit (Prov. 16:18)

Spirit of false doctrines (Ex. 23:1; Matt. 16:12)

Perverse spirit (Isa. 19:14)

Spirit of jealousy (Num. 5:14)

Seducing spirits (I Tim. 4:1)

Sad spirit (I Kings 21:5)

Jealous spirit (Num. 5:14, 30)

Wounded spirit (Prov. 18:14)

Lying spirit (I Kings 22:22-23; II Ch. 18:21-22)

Proud in spirit (Ecc. 7:8)

Spirit of burning (Isa. 4:4)

Familiar spirit (Lev. 20:27; I Sam. 28:7-8; I Ch. 10:13; II Ch. 33:6)

Spirit of Egypt (Isa. 19:3)

Spirit of heaviness (Isa. 61:3)

Spirit of unclean devil (Luke 4:33)

Spirit of the world (I Cor. 2:12)

Timeframe for Deliverance

For some, deliverance can happen instantly, while for most others, it is a process. The process can take months, or it can take years. The difference in timeframe is most likely predicated upon one's mindset and/or how long the ungodly spirit has afflicted him/her. If a person does not see a need to be free from the ungodly spirit or does not recognize its existence, he/she will remain bound for a longer period of time than one who desires the spirit to leave. If the spirit has occupied the person's temple for a while, it will be harder to eradicate the spirit or the residual effects because the person has grown accustomed to operating in a certain manner and may be fearful of change or believe he/she is the way he/she is because that is how God made him/her. This is a lie from the enemy designed to keep one bound. In order to live a fulfilled life, our temples must be free from all ungodly spirits.

To better understand how to begin the process of deliverance, read the two scriptures below:

Matthew 12:43-45 says, *"When an impure spirit comes out of a person, it goes through arid places seeking rest and does not find it. Then it says, 'I will return to the house I left.' When it arrives, it finds the house unoccupied, swept clean and put in order. Then it goes and takes with it seven other spirits more wicked than itself, and they go in and live there. And the final condition of that person is worse than the first. That is how it will be with this wicked generation"* (NIV).

Luke 11:25-26 says, *"When it arrives, it finds the house swept clean and put in order. Then it goes and takes seven other spirits more wicked than itself, and they go in and live there. And the final condition of that person is worse than the first"* (NIV).

Both sets of scripture provide a hint of the first step in being free, but they focus more on the details of the danger the <u>solitary</u> act of expurgating an ungodly spirit from an individual can bring about. As you ponder that statement, I am sure it sounds quite contradictory to all you may have heard about expurgating evil spirits from someone. I am keenly aware of this seeming contradiction. Allow me to explain.

Careful examination of these two sets of verses demonstrate the need for an <u>additional step</u> that must be performed *after* one is delivered from an ungodly spirit. To provide more clarity to this statement, Step One (deliverance) will be discussed in Chapter Two, and Step Two (after deliverance) will be discussed in Chapter Three.

Chapter Two
Step One: The Deliverance Process

As discussed in **Unleashed Anger, Anger Unleashed**, once a person realizes he/she possesses a spirit that is contrary to God's spirit, he/she must take the necessary steps to be delivered from it. Before deliverance begins, you may find it necessary to fast and pray, as Jesus instructed the disciples who complained of not being able to deliver a boy from an evil spirit that possessed him. Read the account below from Mark 9:14-29.

> *When they came to the other disciples, they saw a large crowd around them and the teachers of the law arguing with them. As soon as all the people saw Jesus, they were overwhelmed with wonder and ran to greet him. 'What are you arguing with them about?' he asked. A man in the crowd answered, 'Teacher, I brought you my son, who is possessed by a spirit that has robbed him of speech. Whenever it seizes him, it throws him to the ground. He foams at the mouth, gnashes his teeth and becomes rigid. I asked your disciples to drive out the spirit, but they could not.' 'You unbelieving generation,' Jesus replied, 'how long shall I stay with you? How long shall I put up with you? Bring the boy to me.' So they brought him. When the spirit saw Jesus, it immediately threw the boy into a convulsion. He fell to the ground and rolled around,*

foaming at the mouth. Jesus asked the boy's father, 'How long has he been like this?' 'From childhood,' he answered. 'It has often thrown him into fire or water to kill him. But if you can do anything, take pity on us and help us.' '"If you can"?' said Jesus. 'Everything is possible for one who believes.' Immediately the boy's father exclaimed, 'I do believe; help me overcome my unbelief!' When Jesus saw that a crowd was running to the scene, he rebuked the impure spirit. 'You deaf and mute spirit,' he said, 'I command you, come out of him and never enter him again.' The spirit shrieked, convulsed him violently and came out. The boy looked so much like a corpse that many said, 'He's dead.' But Jesus took him by the hand and lifted him to his feet, and he stood up. After Jesus had gone indoors, his disciples asked him privately, 'Why couldn't we drive it out?' He replied, 'This kind can come out only by prayer' (NIV).

Fasting and praying assists in developing one's faith and strengthening the power God has given us. The stronger our faith, the greater our ability will be to exercise that which God has empowered us to do. Notice from the verses above, all Jesus had to do was speak to the demon and the demon fled from the boy's temple. Jesus knew the power He had, and He exercised it. This same power was given unto the disciples, but they failed in being successful in expurgating the demon. Jesus' response to their failed attempt was, *"You unbelieving generation. How long shall I stay with you? How long shall I put up with you?"* He was disappointed that the disciples had not yet begun to catch on to what they were able to do with the proper faith.

If you have failed in anything, ask yourself where your faith level is. Do you have no faith, little faith, some faith, or great faith? In Matthew 17:10, Jesus declares, *"Because you have so little faith. Truly I tell you, if you have faith as small as a mustard seed, you can say to this mountain, 'Move from here to there,' and it will move. Nothing will be impossible for you."* Your level of faith determines the outcome of that which you are involved. If you believe you will be successful, more than likely you will be. You may not have the level of success you desire after the first attempt, but if you keep at it, you will eventually succeed. However, if you believe you will fail, more than likely you will. This is called the self-fulfilling prophecy, which was heavily discussed by Robert K. Merton, in 1948, and has been used by educational psychologists from that time forward.

The Bible, however, had already given us insight into this principle. Proverbs 23:7a states, *"For as he thinketh in his heart, so is he."* Whatever is going on in our minds will manifest in our lives. So, how do we change our mindset so that we get more positive outcomes? We increase our faith level. How is that done? The answer is provided in Romans 10:17: *"So then faith cometh by hearing, and hearing by the word of God."* We are empowered by increasing our exposure to the *spoken* Word and to the Word in general.

In reading the Word, we are exposed to and enlightened by Luke 10:19, which says, *"Behold, I give unto you power to tread on serpents and scorpions, and over all the power of the enemy: and nothing shall by any means hurt you."* When we know who we are in Christ, then we can begin to use the power we have to walk in freedom from ungodly spirits.

Now, let us examine the process of deliverance. There are six basic steps to your deliverance. Take one step at a time, spending as much time as necessary in each one.

1. *Know what is rightfully yours*

If you don't believe what is rightfully yours, it is going to be hard to state your claim. Some of the things you need to be clear about are 1. knowing your sins are forgiven (although Satan will always try to bring up your past failures), 2. knowing you are a child of God and are a co-heir with the Lord Jesus Christ (Romans 8:17), and 3. knowing you have authority over the demons (Luke 10:19).

-You need to understand who you are in Christ.

This sounds simple, and is often overlooked, but is VITAL to your deliverance. If you don't really believe you are who you are, then you won't have the faith to stand on who you are and claim what is rightfully yours. Think about this- if a child has parents who are able to provide his every financial need but he fails to take advantage of their wealth by making his request known, he will not enjoy the benefits. Likewise, if you don't really know you're a child of the King, you won't feel like a prince or princess, and you won't act like a prince or princess. And how are you supposed to defeat the enemy when you don't think like a child of God should think? If you struggle with your identity, you need to tear down one or more strongholds.

Begin by reading the following verses. II Corinthians 5:17 says, *"Therefore if anyone is in Christ, he is a new creature; the old things passed away; behold, new things have come."* And, I Peter 2:9 says, *"But ye are a chosen generation, a royal priesthood, an holy nation, a peculiar people; that ye should shew forth the praises of him who hath called you out of darkness into his marvellous light."* And, Romans 8:17 says, *"And if children, then heirs; heirs of God, and joint-heirs with Christ; if so be that we suffer with him, that we may be also glorified together."* Now that you have read God's position on your relationship/kinship with Him, you should be clear about your identity.

-You need to know that your sins are forgiven.

If you have guilt hanging over your head, it will greatly hinder your ability to stand up to the enemy with a clear conscience and stand up for what is rightfully yours. Guilt is a door opener and keeper, and the enemy often uses it as a base to launch all sorts of attacks against God's children. You need to understand the nature of God and how freely Jesus wants to forgive you of ALL your sins. Forgiveness, however, is two-fold. First, in order to be forgiven, you must forgive others of their trespasses (Matthew 6:14). The difficulty most people have with forgiveness is placing blame. If they believe someone is at fault, they believe they have every right to be angry, disappointed, hurt, and even upset. I agree. It is their right to experience those emotions when they have been wronged; however, withholding forgiveness is sin. You are to have a heart of compassion. A compassionate heart is not a heart that is hardened;

instead, it is a heart of love. Therefore, you should love others through and past their shortcomings. In doing so, you can offer forgiveness. Afterward when you confess your sins, God is faithful and just to forgive you (I John 1:9), and your prayers will not be hindered.

-You need to have the correct perception of God and your relationship with Him.

If your perception of God is incorrect, you are going to be an easy target for the enemy. If you perceive God as solely a loving god, you will be confused and tormented when things around you don't go as you expect them (the tragedies and natural disasters in the world). On the other hand, if you perceive God to be a judgmental god who only has a wrath, you will walk in fear rather than reverence (honor). God's true identity is two-fold. God can be best characterized as a just god. He is just because He does what is right and what is best in a given situation. When it is time to love, nurture, and encourage, God does that. When it is time to rebuke, chastise, and judge, God does that. God is always fair, for He is no respecter of persons (Acts 10:34; Romans 2:11).

Let's take a quick look at the Israelites. When the time came for their captivity in Egypt to come to an end, God sent His manservant Moses to Pharaoh to demand His people be set free. However, once the Israelites were freed and entered into the wilderness, they murmured, complained, walked in disobedience to God, and committed sinful acts. Because of their abhorrent behaviors, God saw fit for them to wander in the wilderness for forty years until the first generation died off, thereby not being able to enter into the promise land. So, you can see, one god can have both characteristics of being loving and being able to chasten.

Our God is no different from a good parent. A good parent will feed, bathe, and clothe of a child, all while providing shelter. At the same time, the parent will teach the child how to be responsible and self-sufficient, so he/she can function effectively as an adult. But when necessary, the parent will rebuke and chasten the child. This is for the child's betterment. Proverbs 13:24 instructs, *"Those who spare the rod of discipline hate their children. Those who love their children care enough to discipline them"* (NLT).

-You need to know the authority you have been given by God over the enemy.

You, as a believer, have been given authority over all powers of the enemy (Luke 10:19) and have been given the authority to bind and loose in the spiritual realm (Matthew 18:18). You must exercise your authority through the spoken Word in faith. Just as Jesus cast demons out with His Word, you can also cast demons out with your words, which are backed by the authority that Jesus gave us as believers. **Newsflash!!!** You have the authority whether you feel you have it not, as long as you are a believer. It is important to know that your authority is accessed through faith, and therefore the more you believe in your authority, the more of it you will be able to exercise. Mark 16:17 tells us, *"And these signs shall follow them that believe; In my name shall they cast out devils; they shall speak with new tongues."*

You must not take a backseat to the enemy who only wants to wreak havoc in your life. You must stand your ground on the solid foundation of God's Word and declare what you want for your life. Romans 4:17b says, *"calleth those things which be not as though they were."* Just because your present situation may not be exactly what you desire it to be doesn't mean it can't be. God holds the world in His hands. He is the Almighty Creator, and He is in control.

2. Find the open doors and break off any legal grounds

This step is one of the most important parts of the deliverance process. It is important to find out what opened the door to the enemy, so you can close it and void their legal right to inhabit you. There are a number of ways they can gain access: through sins, ancestral sins (which causes ancestral curses), unforgiving heart (which blocks God's forgiveness toward us), dabbling in the occult, demonic vows, fear, etc. Find the door that was open and close it. Ceasing the activity closes the door. The longer you engage in a sinful activity, the longer you give the demons permission to inhabit your body.

3. Identify the areas of bondage in your life

It is important to know what areas of your life are in bondage, so you will know exactly what you are seeking to be set free from. Make a list of the things you want to be freed from. Then try to identify the 'open door' that allowed the enemy to move into that area of your life. When did it start? If you had it your entire life, and your parents or grandparents struggled with the same or similar problem, then it was likely generational. Often you can locate what opened up the door to bondage if you look back around the time in your life when it started.

When I began my deliverance process, I mentally traveled back in time when I believed my personality began to change from my fun-loving, free-spirited girl to a teenager who had built walls around herself and was always on the defense. To ensure I had the timeframe correct, I inquired of my mother when she noticed the change in me. The age we both came up with was eleven years old. Ironically, that was the time I had been molested by my stepfather. The sexual abuse opened the door to the unclean spirit 'anger' and later to the unclean spirit 'murder.' By acknowledging when the change took place, I had a clear understanding of what caused the shift in my life and what needed to be cleared from my temple.

4. Cast the demons out

After determining which spirit(s) are present, take authority over the demon spirits within you by issuing a command such as, "In the name of Jesus, I now take authority over every evil spirit present within me, and I command each and every one to submit to the authority invested in me by Jesus Christ!"

If you can address the demons by name (lust, anger, suicide, hate, fear, etc.), you will often find them submitting to your authority easier because it makes it harder on them to write you off as if you weren't talking to them and as though you have no authority. Demons tremble at the name of Jesus. Recall Acts 19:15 when the demon said, *"Jesus I know, and Paul I know; but who are ye?"* If you don't have the authority in your own name, use the name of Jesus!

If somebody yelled, "Hey you!" in a crowd, you probably wouldn't pay any attention to him. But if he yelled out your name, you would be a lot quicker to respond. The same is true with demons. If you address them by name, it is a lot easier to get their attention. Notice how many times Jesus addressed the demons by name, such as deaf and dumb spirits, etc. (Mark 9:25).

Using your authority in Jesus, command the evil spirits (by name if possible) to come out of you in Jesus' name! Don't be alarmed if you find yourself throwing up all of a sudden, coughing uncontrollably, screaming, etc. If you do, that is a good sign. It usually means they are on their way out!

5. Encountering groupings of demons

Demons often work in teams, and if you identify the strongman, it will help you in figuring out their game plan, and give you a better idea of how to go about casting out certain demons first and unraveling their scheme. This is important, because this strongman is usually the big guy that you are going after. Once you cast him out, the lesser demons usually follow suit much easier. However, sometimes it is better to cast out the lesser demons, and then deal with their leader after they are all gone because he can no longer play games or hide behind them.

As mentioned earlier, I had the unclean spirit of anger and murder. However, those spirits stemmed from the root of bitterness. Also attached to the root of bitterness are hatred, violence, resentment, retaliation, and forgiveness. Read below for other demon groupings. Note- This list by no means is comprehensive.

Depression
despair
despondency
discouragement
defeatism
dejection
hopelessness
suicide
death
insomnia
morbidity

Rebellion
self-will
stubbornness
disobedience
anti-submissiveness

Insecurity
inferiority
self-pity
loneliness
shyness
timidity
inadequacy
ineptness

Jealousy
envy
suspicion
distrust
selfishness

Impatience
agitation
frustration
intolerance
resentment

criticism

Sexual Impurity
lust
masturbation
homosexuality
adultery
fornication
incest
rape
exposure
frigidity
harlotry

Gluttony
nervousness
compulsive
eating
resentment
frustration
idleness
self-pity
self-reward

Pride
ego
vanity
self-righteousness
haughtiness
importance
arrogance

6. Check to see if you are free

You should feel a noticeable relief when the demon(s) have left. However, they may just be hiding and trying to trick you into calling the deliverance a success, only to rear their heads later. Pray and ask the Holy Spirit to reveal to you if there are any demons remaining that need to be cast out, or whether the deliverance was successful. The long term effect after a deliverance is usually your best indicator, but when there have been symptoms of the demon (such as fear, anger, suicidal urges, etc.), then I would expect those to be gone when the deliverance has been successful.

Don't forget to consider that in many cases, deliverance is a process and may not occur in just one session. If strongholds need to be torn down that the demons are hanging onto, they can usually take time as you tear them down. When the spirits leave you though, you should feel the difference and be able to freely walk in your newfound freedom.

As a word of caution, it is easier to cast out demons than it is to discipline your life. The key to your remaining free is to discipline your mind and actions. We will deal with this in more detail in Chapter Four.

Chapter Three
Step Two: After Deliverance

After you have been set free, you can rejoice. I certainly did. After being freed from the spirit of anger, I was happy to take on a new temperament. I noticed remarkable changes and others did as well. But, it is important to not get caught off guard due to your current success and newfound freedom, which is easy to do. Personally, I was always conscious of being steadfast in my deliverance. I did not want to return back to my old self. This is where the second step in the deliverance process comes in.

In Chapter Two, we covered the first step of the deliverance process: identifying and ridding yourself of the unclean spirits. The second step is just as crucial because it ensures you remain delivered. Let's examine it below.

To assist us, let us be reminded of what Matthew 12:43-45 says, *"When an impure spirit comes out of a person, it goes through arid places seeking rest and does not find it. 44 Then it says, 'I will return to the house I left.' When it arrives, it finds the house unoccupied, swept clean and put in order. 45 Then it goes and takes with it seven other spirits more wicked than itself, and they go in and live there. And the final condition of that person is worse than the first. That is how it will be with this wicked generation" (NIV).*

Verse 43 is essentially what happens after Step One has been completed. The spirit has been cast out, and now it wanders around in dry places aimlessly because it has no place to call home. If you do not want the activities described in verses 44-45 to take place in your life, Step Two must be completed. Verses 44 and 45 tell us inexplicably what will occur if the unclean spirit returns back to the house (body) and finds it empty.

Undoubtedly, the spirit does not desire to wander in a dry place. The spirit was comfortable in its home (your body), where it was nice and warm and could have free reign to do what it pleased. Therefore, the spirit will come back to check the condition of its home, to see if it is empty. To the spirit, an empty house is an invitation to come back inside. Consequently, you must take action to fill your temple so the unclean spirit finds it occupied. An occupied temple means there is no vacancy (no room for the spirit and its seven friends, who are characteristically worse).

You may ask, "How do I go about filling my temple, and what do I fill it with? Well, I am going to assume you want your temple filled with pure positive elements versus unclean negative elements. So, how about choosing elements that will lay a solid foundation in your life and lead you in the right direction? What is contrary to the spirit of darkness? The Spirit of Light. John 8:12 says, *"Then spake Jesus again unto them, saying, I am the light of the world: he that followeth me shall not walk in darkness, but shall have the light of life."*

To have Jesus in your life to be the light, you must first understand and receive the following verse, *"But without faith it is impossible to please him: for he that cometh to God must believe that he is, and that he is a rewarder of them that diligently seek him"* (Hebrews 11:6). You must know that God exists and is a rewarder of those who seek Him. To know He exists is to have faith.

How do you build your faith? Romans 10:17, says, *"So then faith cometh by hearing, and hearing by the word of God."* You must position yourself to hear God's Word. There are many ways to hear the Word of God. The most traditional way is to attend worship services to hear the preached Word. Proceeding with the presumption that you are already a believer, I can assume you probably already attend church services. However, there is a marked difference between simply attending services to hear the spoken Word versus hearing the spoken Word and allowing it to permeate your being. Hebrews 4:12 says, *"For the word of God is quick, and powerful, and sharper than any two-edged sword, piercing even to the dividing asunder of soul and spirit, and of the joints and marrow, and is a discerner of the thoughts and intents of the heart."*

God's Word can transform your life, if you allow it to. In the ten years that have passed since my deliverance experience, I have allowed the Word to transform my life. What I now know about God compared to what I knew then has vastly increased. But the increase in my spiritual awareness didn't occur by accident. I had to purpose in my heart to draw closer to God. Ten years ago, I wasn't a babe in Christ, but I wasn't mature either. It wasn't until I began to fully commune and sup with God that I began to know Him in His fullness. But, first I had to have a desire to do so.

Let me give you an overview of my walk with the Lord, starting with my acceptance of the Lord Jesus Christ as my savior. Notice the change in my activities and the increase in my responsibilities as they relate to ministry.

1984 (age 16) - On my sixteenth birthday, I walked down to the altar and gave my life to Christ (after being consistently raised in church since my birth). Prior to accepting the Lord and getting baptized on my sixteenth birthday, I had experienced a burning desire to do so for the two to three years prior. When I approached my grandmother about wanting to accept Christ, she and my mother discussed it and decided I wasn't ready. I, of course, did not agree, but I had no choice but to accept their decision.

However, on my sixteenth birthday, as I sat in service and listened to the preacher minister God's Word, I felt the same desire that I had been experiencing for the last two to three years. I felt I could no longer be apart from God. I knew He was calling me to come to Him. So, I made up my mind that Christ would be mine, and I would be His.

At the end of the service, when the "invitation" was given, I quietly rose from my seat and politely said to my grandmother, "Excuse me." She was sitting between me and the aisle. She moved her legs to let me pass, and I made my way to the center aisle and proceeded to walk to the altar. I dared not look back at her because I didn't want her to call me back to my seat. I kept marching toward Jesus. I was a young woman determined to connect with her Lord.

1996 (age 28) - After having sat in church for twelve years since my baptism, quietly taking in the Word, I stopped going to church for approximately three years. I had relocated my residence (consequently leaving my church of ten years), and I sporadically began searching for a church home. During the three years that I did not have a church home, my spirit constantly longed for God. I felt a void, and I desperately wanted it filled. However, I wasn't steadfastly looking for a church home.

1999 (age 31) - I found a church home, re-committed my life to God, and re-introduced my two sons, who were six and nine years old, to a spiritually driven life. Like me, my sons had been in church since they were born. But, our absence from church caused a void for all of us.

2001 (age 33) - I re-developed the Children's Church Ministry at my church. Some time prior to my joining the church, there had been a children's ministry in place, but for some reason it had dissolved. I took great pride and joy in re-establishing that ministry and teaching the children every Sunday morning. I filled the room with supplies and arts and crafts, and the children and I had a blast talking about God.

2005 (age 37) - I was delivered from the anger that had plagued my life for 26 years, after learning about forgiveness and forging a deeper relationship with God. For the last six years, I had really begun to hunger and thirst for righteousness. At that time, I attended church approximately three days a week. I attended Sunday school, midweek service, leaders meetings, and Sunday worship. I also attended every event that occurred in between, such as conferences and other special church services. In the past, I had attended Sunday worship services and Bible study, but I never felt quite the way I felt once I returned to church while I was away for the three-year period. I felt lost. I felt a great void in my life. When I reconnected with God, I vowed to never have that feeling of emptiness again. So for the last sixteen years, I have been walking closely with the Lord.

2006 - I founded International Women's Commission. It is a ministry that seeks to develop the entire person by focusing on aspects of spirituality, education, finances, health, sexuality, and healing and deliverance. I also became a licensed minister of the gospel of Jesus Christ.

2007 - I became involved with the Sunday school ministry by teaching college-age students. At my church, the Sunday school ministry was being re-organized, and my pastor asked me to teach the college-age students. At that time, I had been teaching college-age students in my profession as an English professor for seven years, so I felt comfortable teaching them at church as well. Consequently, I accepted the assignment.

2009 - After teaching the college-age Sunday school class, my class eventually dissolved. So, I began attending the adult Sunday school class and would from time to time assist in teaching the class. Eventually, the person who was teaching the course handed it over to me, and I became the adult Sunday school teacher. I still teach that class today (co-teaching with my husband).

2010 - At my church, the men held a 'men's only' session on Wednesday night prior to Bible study. During that session, the men would discuss topics that relate solely to men. And, they would survey the topics through the lens of the Word of God. I was so intrigued by the session that I thought it would be a good idea if the women had something similar to discuss women's issues. I mentioned my idea to the pastor's wife, our co-pastor, and she told me to go ahead and start it. I didn't feel one hundred percent comfortable taking on another assignment, so I held still. A couple of months later, she started the group, and a month later, she turned it right over to me. Our women's group was called *Wisdom from Above*. It remained in session for four years. It was a great success with the women because they had a forum where they could release and share what was on their hearts and receive godly counsel. Maybe our pastor will re-institute it one day.

2012 - I became the director of the Institute Bible Classes, which is an educational biblical program, consisting of seven courses.

2014 - I was assigned to be the chaplain and treasurer of the Redeemed Women's Ministry.

During the ten years since my deliverance, I drew closer to God by staying in His Word. I attended worship services, I read and studied His Word, and I taught and preached His Word. Today, I continue all of those activities, as I desire to continue to draw closer to my Father.

One's increase in responsibility is *usually* commensurate with his/her increase in spiritual maturity. God knows what is inside of me, and He knows He can trust me with His people. Therefore, He allows me the privilege of teaching, ministering, and overseeing a portion of the flock.

When any believer makes great strides in his/her relationship with God, God will begin to use him/her to further the gospel. Furthering the gospel is a part of worshipping God. Worshipping God is our sole purpose for existing. Let's discuss worship for a moment.

I found the following excerpt on worship from Pastor Jack Hayford to be very insightful:

Worship has often been misunderstood as the musical prelude to the sermon, rather than the means by which we, as the people of God, invite the dominion of His Kingdom to be established on earth.

Psalm 22:3 says that the King of kings is literally "enthroned" in our praises. Wherever God's people come together to worship, we become a habitation for His presence. God comes to dwell where His people worship, and where that happens, all the weight of His glory, His rulership, and His dominion are present. In this atmosphere—where worship ushers in the presence of God—four critically important things take place: first, the Word becomes life, not just an intellectual exercise; then, as His Kingdom is established, people will be healed and people will come to know the Lord. Finally, because God is empowering His people, their worship crowds out the borders of hell's current domain—Satan having been given rulership of this planet by man's forfeit of dominion at the Fall.

Worship is essential to God's plan of redemption and provides a strategic avenue for God's entry into an alienated world. An illustration of this is found in the Lord's Prayer, which begins with worship: "Our Father in heaven, hallowed be Your name." Then, it extends the invitation "…Your kingdom come, Your will be done on earth as it is in heaven" (Matthew 6:9, 10). When we pray in the manner that Jesus taught His disciples, we are first, with worship, reaching into the invisible realm and then, on the grounds of our worship, welcoming the entry of His divine authority, rulership, and power into this world.

How then, do we worship?

After giving the Ten Commandments, the Lord gave explicit directions to Moses about building a tabernacle of worship in which He would come to dwell among His people (Exodus 25:8, 9). The people spent a year at Sinai building the tabernacle according to God's pattern and learning how to worship. God's plan for His people's redemption was to be realized through the priestly ministry of worship. In Christ, all believers have become a "royal priesthood" that we "may proclaim the praises of Him who called [us] out of the darkness unto His marvelous light" (1 Peter 2:9).

The biblical patterns of worship involve all aspects of the human personality: physical, emotional, intellectual, and spiritual. Most people recognize that worship ought to be spiritual from the heart and that it ought to be intelligent.

But there's uneasiness about the involvement of our emotions and physical expression. Yet people who acknowledge their own physical and emotional being before the Lord do what in any setting other than church would be considered the most natural thing. The living God has created us with a response mechanism that expresses joy when we are happy, or elation and shouting over victory, for example.

The expression of worship should not be confused as a requirement for salvation, but as a means for truth springing to life in the midst of people. When we surrender ourselves to the full expression of worship, the Spirit descends, and room is given for Him to meet every person in a special way.

Worship involves physical expressions founded upon biblical guidelines; they are neither ritual, perfunctory actions, nor the serving of emotions for their own sake. Among the physical expressions of worship found in Scripture are kneeling, clapping hands, raising hands, verbalized praise, singing hymns and psalms, weeping, laughing, bearing witness aloud ("Amen"), reading the Word aloud, prostrating before the Lord, speaking in tongues, dancing before the Lord, giving public testimony, standing, silence, and spiritual song. In just a single chapter (20) of 2 Chronicles, eleven different Hebrew verbs for active physical worship are found.

In his epistle to the Romans, the Apostle Paul proclaims the glory of our Lord and the motivation for our worship: "Oh, the depth of the riches both of the wisdom and knowledge of God! How unsearchable are His judgments and His ways past finding out!... For of Him and through Him and to Him are all things, to whom be glory forever. Amen" (11:33-36). And then he summons us to worship with what can be considered our only appropriate response to such magnificence: "I beseech you therefore, brethren, by the mercies of God, that you present your bodies a living sacrifice, holy, acceptable to God, which is your reasonable service. And do not be conformed to this world, but be transformed by the renewing of your mind, that you may prove what is that good and acceptable and perfect will of God" (12:1, 2).

Thus, the Bible calls us to: Present our rededicated bodies by kneeling, bowing, raising our heads and hands, and dancing before the Lord; present our revived emotions by shouting and clapping to the Lord, praising aloud, rejoicing, and expressing thanksgiving, or by being silent before Him in the beauty of His presence; present our regenerated spirits by worshipping in the Spirit, singing spiritual songs, and giving thanks; and present our renewed minds by obedient, orderly, intelligent, sensitive worship with understanding. Even spontaneity must have some point of discipline and control (see 1 Corinthians 14:40).

The Lord is not displeased by our reticence to the physical expressions of worship, but when we present ourselves wholly open before Him, the compounding of both our life in Him and of His beauty in us takes place. We are made more whole—and holy—in the likeness of Jesus. The weight of His glory begins to seep through our system. Our identity becomes more secure and established, and our sense of sufficiency in the life of Jesus Christ increases.

The Lord says in Romans 14:11 that one day, every knee shall bow and every tongue shall confess Him. Therefore, we are summoned to present our bodies, emotions, spirits, and minds to Him in every biblical form of expression as He would graciously teach us. And when we worship as His appointed "priests," we invite and administrate His glorious life, purpose, and power to be realized not only in our lives, but also in our world. (Hayford, 2011)

What profound words shared by Pastor Hayford. I was truly moved, and I pray you were also and that you have a better understanding of how to worship God and why we should worship Him!

Chapter Four
Evidence of Deliverance

It is one thing for the Holy Spirit to identify an unclean spirit or legion of spirits that resides in one's own temple, but it is quite another to know when God has expurgated the unclean spirit(s) because the residual effects that linger afterward can cause a person to believe the spirit(s) is/are still there. Think about this, if you break your leg and are required to wear a cast for six weeks, your walking pattern will change from what it was before. Once the cast has been removed, it is not likely that you will immediately return to walking as normal. Most likely you will still continue to favor the newly healed leg because for six weeks that is what you did. It takes a while to adjust back to normal and treat the leg as you once did prior to the break.

Here is another example: There are two people who have a tumultuous relationship because there is always arguing and fighting. Each time the two prepare to see one another, they are on edge because they know their normal pattern of interaction. And, they prepare for what they consider to be inevitable. One day, the nature of their relationship changes, and as a result, the element of arguing is removed. A few weeks or a month later, the two individuals plan to see each other. As the hour grows near for them to actually meet, they both grow nervous due to their past experiences with each other. Just because they feel nervous and are anxious about their meeting does that mean things will go awry when they see each other? Of course not. Their meeting may go perfectly smoothly, but until they learn to operate differently or have greater expectations of their interaction, they may continue to feel awkward in each other's presence.

Here is a third example to illustrate my perspective. There was a married couple whose relationship was very harmonious because each one fulfilled specific roles in the marriage and everything operated as a well-oiled machine. Until one day when God took the husband to his eternal resting place. He was the one who was responsible for the financial stability of the home. He paid the bills and attended to all the financial matters of their household. After he passed, his wife understood she needed to assume his roles as well as maintain her own. However, *knowing and doing is two different things*. It actually took her two months before she changed her behavior patterns. Even when the late notices came and the threatening phone calls were received, she still didn't change immediately. She actually had to wrap her mind around changing her old behaviors to new behaviors that would prove more beneficial for her livelihood. Eventually, this is exactly what she did, and then she was able to function more effectively.

This same concept can be applied to how one's personality is altered when an unclean spirit is present in his/her temple. Generally speaking, the longer the spirit was present, the longer it will take the person to return to normal. For example, when a spirit causes a person to be defensive towards others, even when the spirit is no longer present, the person may still automatically act defensively toward others until he/she purposes to act differently. Basically what I am saying is a person's behavior patterns that were dictated by or a result of the presence of an unclean spirit can remain, as a matter of habit, even after the unclean spirit is gone.

At some point, a person who has had an unclean spirit removed must begin to show outward signs of deliverance. You must believe that God has cleaned your temple and act accordingly. Here are two verses that will assist you in changing your behavior patterns.

1. As a man thinketh so is he (Proverbs 23:7a). You will be what you think you are. If you say you are free and healed, walk in that freedom. Be the new creature in Christ that you profess you are.

2. Speak those things that be not as though they were (Romans 4:17). Even though you may not feel completely changed and free, but you know God delivered you, speak life into your situation. If you believe in your heart that you are free, confess it regardless of whether you are showing outward signs or not.

****

Let's briefly revisit my deliverance from uncontrollable anger, so I can demonstrate with real-life examples how the outward demonstration of being free from an unclean spirit can be or appear.

Personally, I believe I was in denial for many years about my uncontrollable anger. I knew I had a temper, but I did not sit and watch it grow overtime and worsen. I was otherwise engaged in life. Therefore, I did not detect the severity of it. However, whether I paid attention to its growth and development or not, my uncontrollable temper and rage *did* grow. Unfortunately, the spirit increased in intensity.

Many of my family members would make mention of my bad attitude, but they did so in a condescending manner rather than in a manner that was helpful. The attitude behind the comments said, "You can change if you want to." I found that general perspective to be untrue. At times, I did want to change, but unknowingly I had given power over to the unclean spirit. When my family made their comments, they only made me more hostile. As time passed, my episodes of uncontrollable anger began to occur more frequently (instead of every few years to yearly, then monthly). At the same time, however, I became more spiritually inclined, and I began to understand what was taking place within me, why it was taking place, and how it came to be.

The next step for me was to decide whether or not I wanted to continue along the destructive path I was on or whether or not I wanted to allow the Holy Spirit to deliver me from my uncontrollable anger. Well, as you have already read in the last chapter- I decided I wanted to be free. But actually being free and wanting to be free is really two different things. First, the desire for freedom is necessary. As we know, God gives us free will, and He will not come in and remove any unclean spirits from us unless we have a desire for them to be gone. Once we give the Holy Spirit the right of way in our lives, then the deliverance process can begin.

However, complete deliverance is a process, just like sanctification. The spirit can be called out and subsequently be removed immediately, or it can take some time after one fasts and prays to strengthen his/her resolve. Afterwards, a person's behaviors need to change. When my deliverance process began, I knew without a shadow of a doubt God had delivered me from anger. However, that spirit had resided within me for approximately twenty-five to twenty-six years. So, you can imagine the mindset and behaviors I had acquired during that time frame. So, after the spirit left, I never claimed to be 100% delivered from the effects of anger because I couldn't say what I would do or what I wouldn't do at any given time and know that I would be 100% accurate. And, I didn't want to appear to be something I wasn't.

Having the spirit of anger expurgated was the beginning of my deliverance process. But as the years went by, I began to notice a great change in my temperament. At that point, it was easy for me to say how I felt about certain incidences that would have angered me before my deliverance. Incidentally, I still was very careful about saying I was completely delivered from uncontrollable anger. I wasn't 100% sure where I stood because I had not been placed in any situations that would cause me to blow things out of proportion or act out of control. However, as fate would have it, incidents would come my way that would show others and me where I truly stood with my anger.

Next, you will read one occurrence that took place about three years after my deliverance and then three occurrences that took place five to six years after that (eight to nine years after my deliverance). I will explain how I handled each incident to show you the progression in the change in my behavior pattern and how the Holy Spirit truly rid me of the effects of uncontrollable anger and rage. Not only will I explain my responses to each situation, but I will also explain how I would have responded to the same situation in times past when I was still bound.

Incident #1 (Behavior Patterns Still Lingering)

On one Sunday, in 2009, during the morning worship service, my eldest son walked into the church and asked me to come outside. I didn't know what the problem was, but I rose from my seat and followed him outside. When I made it outside and inquired about the problem, my son informed me that one of the female church members approached him and had words with him and his girlfriend and her words had offended them. Because my son was only eighteen at the time and the woman was older than I was, I felt the need to approach her to see exactly what the problem was.

From the moment I approached her, she was very hostile. She really didn't want to talk to me. She was very rude and began making threats towards me and my husband, telling me she was going to send someone to the church to beat his ass. She also informed me that she knew my ex-husband, and she knew where I lived. I wasn't the least bit intimidated. As a matter of fact, her words made me want to retaliate. So, I kept walking towards her as I made responses to let her know her words didn't scare me. We made a scene in the church parking lot, but my husband stood between us to keep a physical altercation from ensuing. I remember repeatedly saying, "I just want to talk to her." My husband told me, "You can't try to reason with those kind of people."

I guess my feelings were mixed. On one hand, I wanted to find out what she had said that offended my son. On the other hand, due to her hostility and her reputation of being very rude to people, I wanted to let her know without a shadow of a doubt that I was not one she could bully.

When I discussed the incident with others, I told them, "No one messes with my children." I felt wholeheartedly that I had the right to protect them, and I wouldn't permit anyone to tell me otherwise. The truth of the matter is, what I was sharing with everyone was true, but at the same time I had probably taken things a little further than needed. But, I was fine with it. I wasn't making any excuses for my behavior.

However, when I reviewed the situation years later, I saw reflections of the old me, and I regretted my actions. I told myself there was probably a better way to have handled the situation.

Five years later, in 2014, a second incident occurred. Read the account below.

Incident #2 (The Holy Spirit at Work)

In March 2014, I wrote a novel titled *A Touch in the Dark*. From the novel, I also wrote a play. The play was a gift to my church to be used as a fundraiser for my pastor and wife's 40th year of ministry. As I directed the play, there were approximately twenty-two actors involved. From what I could tell, everyone was pleased to be involved in the play, with the exception of one particular actress. She was excited too, yet disgruntled at the same time, which became more and more evident by the comments she would make during rehearsals.

On one particular Saturday, while we were rehearsing, the disgruntled actress, whom I will call April, had a serious outburst. The outburst came directly after I was taking time out to give instructions to one of the other actresses. The one actress that I was speaking directly to had the same role as April, so I guess what I was saying to her as far as correction April took to heart as well. April immediately jumped in and started complaining about how I spoke to the cast members and said I was disrespectful and rude and that I spoke to them as if though they were children. She also said I put them down and when I put them down, she was not going to allow herself to stay put down, but she would lift herself back up.

I was shocked and appalled at what she was accusing me of, but I quietly listened to what she had to say. When she was done speaking, I began to respond by telling her, "It is never my intent to put anyone down, and if that's what I have done, I sincerely apologize. It is only my intent to push all of you to the level at which I know you can perform." My words were not uttered because I was in agreement with her comment about me putting people down. It was quite the contrary. I am cognizant that people see things differently, and I believe they have a right to their own impressions. Therefore, I apologized to keep the peace rather than try to defend myself. When a person is headstrong, like Alice, it is difficult to convince them their opinion is not accurate.

However, in the midst of my response, April interrupted me several times, cutting me off to continue on with her banter. Finally, one of the other cast members interrupted and began to speak, to try to get a handle on the situation, which was becoming increasingly volatile. Also, my husband, who was in the skybox, came down because he was also witnessing the growing tension. At that moment, I excused myself and walked out of the room, into another part of the church. I needed desperately to catch my breath because I couldn't understand what had gone wrong when we were preparing for what was such a good cause.

When I walked into the back room of the church, two or three women followed me and began to let me know that I had their full support and that they were deeply angered and troubled by the incident that had just occurred. They were telling me things, such as, "Who does she think she is?" "She has not walked in your shoes to get to where you are." "I don't know why she's trying to be you." Etc. Etc.

After I recomposed myself, I walked back into the sanctuary, where practice was being held, to explain my perspective and my entire outlook as far as the play was concerned. When I returned to the cast of actors, I calmly explained to them that the story they were acting out was actually a part of my life story and the play was so much bigger than all of us because it would render healing and deliverance to anyone in the audience who so needed it, it would bring glory and honor to God, and it would be uplifting for our pastor and his wife. I also informed them that the reason they were in the play was because I saw something in them and I was determined to pull it out and by no means would I ever tell them they were doing a fantastic job when in actuality they were not. I informed them I would always be honest with them and if I was pushing them, it wasn't my intent to be harsh, but it was for their betterment and for the good of the play.

The cast member, who had brought a halt to the discussion earlier, stepped in and said, "You know Dr. C. works in the spirit of excellence. We are here to support her and do our best." At the end of the rehearsal on that day, all of the cast members, myself, and my husband gathered in a circle, held hands, and prayed. After everyone had departed the sanctuary, April walked up to me and said, "I apologize. It wasn't you. It's me. I know I didn't study my lines, and I was just trying to make excuses to get out of it." I looked at her and said okay. Then, she departed.

I was really disappointed that the incident had occurred. I really don't appreciate when people take their shortcomings out on me and try to make me the bad guy when in essence they have shortcomings they have not come to terms with. It puts a strain on our relationship, if we have one, or it prevents a true relationship from developing because I know they are harboring something in their heart towards me.

The only thing I wanted to do with the play was to do something that was pleasing to God, to uplift His name, and bring glory and honor to Him. That was my only intent. It was not to make a name for myself or to brag about any talents and gifts I possess because I know they all come from Him. I am always mindful to give Him all the glory, praise and honor for what He has done and is doing in my life.

In the past, I would have responded to the actress in a completely different way. I would have walked directly up to her face, met fire with fire, and would have outdone anything she could have ever thought she would have done to me.

However, I did not feel in any way like I wanted to respond in that manner. Instead, I took the humble and meek road. The situation called for humility and for being an example before all of the witnesses and before God as well. And, I felt perfectly content with how I handled the situation.

In December 2014, another incident occurred. Read the following account:

Incident #3 (God has the Upper Hand)

One Sunday at church, as the director over one of the educational programs, I was scheduled to award certificates to various students who had completed a series of classes. Their certificates were to be awarded at the end of the morning worship service. During the service, as the pastor preached his morning sermon, I went through the certificates and applied my signature to each and every one of them. As I did so, the Holy Spirit spoke to me and told me to say these words before awarding any certificates, "If I miss anyone's name, please let me know, and we will correct the situation right away." However, by the time the sermon ended and I was given the floor to call the students' names, the words the Holy Spirit had said to me completely vanished from my mind. Unfortunately, I would pay for that oversight later.

After I had awarded all of the certificates and had taken my seat, the service ended shortly thereafter. Not two minutes later, one of the instructors within the program came up to me and informed me that I had overlooked one of her students. I looked up at her from my seat, and I said very lightheartedly, "It's okay. We will fix it. We have more certificates and more ink in the printer." She responded, "Oh, okay. I will let her know."

A few minutes later, I shifted gears and went about fulfilling another duty that I had to take care of that particular Sunday. In the midst of fulfilling the duty, I had to make a trip to my car. On my way, I walked by the student whose name I had overlooked, and she was engaged in deep conversation with her instructor. I paid the conversation no attention and went about fulfilling the duty. Moments later, I had to return to my vehicle once again, and as I proceeded to do so, I walked past one of the associate pastors who asked me, "Did you speak to Mary?" Mary was the disgruntled student. I told her, "No, but someone did speak to me on Mary's behalf." She proceeded to tell me Mary was upset, and I said, "I'm sure she is," because I knew Mary's temperament. The associate pastor stopped me, by touching me lightly on my arm, and said, "No, she is extremely upset. Her husband came to me and said she stormed out of the church cursing." I said, "Oh, really? She is standing right outside, so let me go talk to her now." The associate pastor said to me, "You can't reason with an angry man." I assured her everything would be okay.

When I stepped outside, Mary and her instructor were still engaged in conversation. I walked over and said, "Excuse me. I need to interrupt for a moment." As soon as I said that, Mary went off the deep end and yelled, "No! I do not want to talk to you! I don't have anything to say to you! Stay away from me!" Before I could respond, Mary's husband walked up to her and said, "You need to talk to her." But, Mary responded, "No, I don't have anything to say to her. If the 40th anniversary wasn't enough, this is it! I told you it is personal!" Her husband responded in disagreement and said, "It is not personal." I approached her and said, "It is definitely not personal." In disagreement with me, she responded, "Oh, no! It's personal," as she glared at me with an evil stare.

I stood there bewildered, wondering what was really going on because I knew she could not be upset simply due to the oversight of her name and not being awarded a certificate. I knew there was a deeper issue because of the short phrases she was saying. As I stood there with my mouth agape and my mind racing around the track, her husband was desperately trying to get her to have a conversation with me to clear up the misunderstanding. Finally, Mary acquiesced and said, "If she wants to speak to me on a one-on-one basis that's fine." I said, with a bit of sarcasm, "Well, that's what I'm trying to do." I continued to approach them, as they continued to back away in the opposite direction.

Shortly after, when her husband realized our conversation was attracting attention from other congregants, he suggested that he and she move inside the church. Shortly after that, I followed them into one of the classrooms. As soon as I stepped inside, Mary looked at me and yelled, "What is she doing here? I don't have anything to say to her! I am going home!" She then grabbed her keys off the table. I thought her behavior and outburst were quite odd because she had just consented to speaking to me on a one-on-one basis. At that point, it seemed as if though my attempts to converse with her were futile.

Once again her husband prevented her from leaving, as he tried to calm her down and be the voice of reason. Meanwhile, I just stood there still bewildered, as I wondered what was really happening. I had no idea that the interaction that we had had in the past had come to that point. Things were really boiling over- for her at least. I was as calm as a cucumber.

Meanwhile, as I was lost in my own thoughts, I heard her mention something to her husband about four years things had been going on between her and me. I stood in utter disbelief because I had not even known her for four years. Sure, we had been at the same church, but I didn't know who she was, nor had I spoken to her to my knowledge. My first recollection of knowing who she was was when I had published her book, which was only two years prior.

Finally, she calmed down enough to want to talk to me after I told her I wanted to talk to her so she could express to me what her concerns were. She started by telling me that I should have called her name that morning because she had completed two classes in the program and that she was aware I had received her name from her instructor. After listening to her, I agreed she was correct. I had indeed received her name from her instructor. However, I had misplaced her instructor's list and was going strictly from memory. My honesty didn't sit well with her. She acted as if though it was a trumped up lie and that I was purposefully withholding her certificate from her.

What I wanted her to understand at that moment was that I am only human and all humans are prone to err. Although I operate in the spirit of excellence, it does not mean that I am without fault and will not have an oversight occasionally. I will *not often* have oversights, but occasionally *one* may occur.

After I saw she was not accepting my reasoning, I asked her what else seemed to be the problem because I was not going to stand there and try to convince her that I was telling the truth. In short, I was ready to move on to another topic. So, she took me back to the month prior and told me that she and her husband were involved in one of the special services that was held at the church. During the special service, several pictures were taken and would possibly be placed into a souvenir book.

She was upset because I was the one creating the souvenir book, and supposedly I had flat out refused to include her picture in the book. Again, she took that as a personal attack from me upon her. However, it was at my discretion as to which pictures would be included in the book and if the truth is told, I did not have a picture of her. That is not to say that she didn't take part in the special service or her picture was not taken, but if it were, it was not given to me. Therefore, I just didn't have a picture to even choose from even if I had wanted to. Therefore, I had not purposefully left her out. Furthermore, most of the people who were in the souvenir book paid to be in the book, and all the other pictures were chosen randomly. But, of course, I could not get her to believe my position on that either.

Eventually, she stormed out of the room and told me I needed to be saved, I was only about money, and she had come to my publishing company to get her book published when she could have gone to so many other places. As she was storming out, I questioned her by asking, "This is the spirit of the Lord that you are operating in?" In a deep voice, she screamed, "Oh yeah, because if I wasn't, it would be a whole lot worse!" I retorted, "I'm sure it would be," as I watched her storm out.

At that point, Mary was already out of the room and in the hallway. Her husband was standing outside the door. After his wife stormed out, he began to apologize profusely to me. I told him, "There is no need for you to apologize. God will deal with her."

Afterward, I was in a state of shock, but I still had the other duty to fulfill, so I immediately carried on with my day as usual and fulfilled my other task. However, when I stopped being busy, I felt the shock kick into high gear, and I felt the need for prayer. At that point, I sought out one of the associate pastors, but to my dismay the second service had already begun. Therefore, both associate pastors were fulfilling their responsibilities. Still desiring prayer, I sought out one of my instructors, who just happened to be Mary's instructor, and my husband. They came into the classroom, I sat down, and they prayed for me. As they prayed for me, the tears ran down my face because inside I was disappointed about the accusations that were hurled at me. But at the same time, I felt God doing a work in me.

After the prayer was over, I walked across the hall to the bathroom and promptly cleaned my face. As I was cleaning my face, I heard the Spirit of the Lord say to me, "You are right where I want you to be." Then, I heard the scripture, *"Touch not my anointed and do my prophets no harm"* (Psalm 105:15).

At that point, I continued on with my day. About an hour and a half later, after the second service, one of the associate pastors was passing by me and said, "I understand you were looking for me earlier." I said, "Yes, I was in need of prayer." He immediately said, "No problem. Let's pray." Back into the same classroom we went. I told him that I was in a verbal altercation with one of the members. He stopped and said, "I am going to pray the peace of God, but before I do let me say this- there are a lot of people jealous of you." I simply nodded my head, and he commenced to pray.

As he prayed the peace of God into my life, I received every word of his prayer. Again, the tears ran down my face. Immediately afterwards, I found myself in the ladies' room again cleaning my face. I felt completely relieved in the Lord because I knew that I was in right standing with Him. No thoughts of murder ran through my mind. No thoughts of revenge or retaliation were experienced, and there was no itching in my hand. (Let me explain the itching sensation. In the past, just before I became physically violent, I would experience itching in my hand. That was a sure sign that someone was about to get hit.)

At that point when I didn't feel any of the above sensations or have any destructive thoughts, I knew I had truly been set free and delivered from the explosive anger that once plagued my life. I rejoiced in Him, and immediately, I began to share my testimony with any and everyone who would listen to it.

Side bar- Later that evening, when my husband and I were driving home, he questioned me about the tears I shed as I was being prayed for. He was a little ticked off because he thought I was crying because the lady had verbally assaulted me. He was sorely mistaken. I was crying because I had seen the growth in myself. Yes, I was hurt. But, I rarely shed tears due to being hurt. I was not crying because she *had* hurt me but because I could actually *feel* hurt. When I was walking in anger, not much hurt me. Incidents would only anger me and make me want to retaliate. Being hurt was not something I had allowed myself to feel. To me, being hurt meant I was vulnerable, and I never allowed myself to be vulnerable when it came to my emotions.

Incident #4 (Staying Delivered)

One Saturday morning at 4:30 a.m., as I was resting well- that is sleeping soundly- I heard a slight buzz. A few seconds later, there was another buzz. Because I am a light sleeper, the buzzing sound caused me to awaken immediately. Without opening my eyes or turning over, I reached over and grabbed my cell phone, as I wondered who could be calling or texting me at that hour of the morning. As the phone continued to buzz, I realized there was an incoming text message. As I opened the cover of my cell phone, with squinted eyes, I was very anxious to know who was texting me at that ungodly hour.

Looking at the text message, I saw that it was one of the members from church. My first thought was something must have occurred because the text was from someone who was close to me. But as I began to read the long text message that was broken into several parts, I realized something certainly had occurred, but it was nothing of an emergency or urgent matter. Instead, I was being questioned about why I was taking assignments from her by going to various leaders and/or the pastor and complaining about her services and requesting the assignments be given to me instead.

My immediate response was to let her know that I had not requested any of her assignments nor had I spoken to anyone regarding any of them. Then, I asked her why I would want any more assignments from our church. My hands were full. My church keeps me pretty busy as the Special Events Coordinator, the director over the Institute Hour, the chaplain, treasurer, and a cabinet member of the Redeemed Women's Fellowship, one of the Sunday school teachers, and one of the ministers on the roster. Should I say more? I don't have much time in my schedule to do anything else, with all of the other responsibilities that I carry in my personal life. So, why would I ever ask for somebody else's jobs?

At the same time, however, I was very much aware that her assignments had been taken from her and given to me, but from my understanding she was the cause of losing the responsibilities because she did not complete what she had been asked to do or either because she had a foul attitude while doing them. Even with the knowledge I had, I did not engage in the conversation with her. I told her she needed to speak to those with the power to make such decisions. It was not my place to discuss anything with her.

Once I sent my response back, I received two or three more responses, as the conversation persisted. I was told to run back and tell the pastor about our conversation. At that point, I thought I was being accused of being a gossip. That really bothered me because I do not make it my business to share other people's business that has nothing to do with me. So, I retorted, "I have never shared any confidence with you about anyone else nor have I broken any confidence that you have ever shared with me. So, exactly what do you mean by your comment?" Her response said she wasn't accusing me of being a gossip. None of what she had said made any sense to me whatsoever.

I finally ended the conversation about an hour later by stating I was going to go back to sleep, and I suggested that the sender do the same. Also, I told her I was very surprised that our relationship had gotten to the point of my being accused of doing devilment towards her. She said she felt weird about it too because I am one of the few people that she is close to at the church. To say the least, I wasn't feeling close at that moment.

The incident left me feeling very weird. I was hurt because the accusations were coming from someone whom I considered to be a friend. I lay awake replaying the conversation over and over in my mind, and I woke my husband up and told him about it because it bothered me so much.

But the reason I'm sharing this incident is because of my response. I responded to her with love, regardless of how I felt. Not once did I disrespect her, nor did I want to retaliate. I only wanted to understand exactly what her situation was and how she felt about it. At the same time though, even though I did not want to retaliate, I refuse to be anyone's doormat.

Therefore, after the incident, I felt it would be best to retreat and have little interaction with her because that was not the first time an incident of that nature had occurred between us, nor was it the first time I had witnessed that type of attitude from her directed towards other people. I simply refused to put myself in a situation where I would be knowingly victimized. That is something I would definitely not sign up for. In the past, I would have quickly discontinued the texting and made a phone call. I would have asked her what her problem was, and I would have accused her of losing her mind. Furthermore, I would have been short on patience and would have raised my voice several octaves (which I'm still able to do). The reason I did not respond in that manner is because with God I have developed a measure of patience and the fruit of the Spirit.

I shared these four incidents to demonstrate the progression of a change in one's mindset. Being delivered from an unclean spirit does not mean automatic deliverance from behaviors. This process is not something that should be taken lightly, nor is it a process that can be rushed. We should definitely confess our healing and deliverance when it comes to dealing with unclean spirits just as we would if we were dealing with an illness. We must declare the works of the Lord, even when we haven't witnessed the full manifestation of them yet. We must know that God is not a man that He should lie (Numbers 23:19) and trust that His Word will not return unto Him void but accomplish that for which it had been sent (Isaiah 55:11).

Chapter 5
Maintaining Deliverance

Once the unclean spirit(s) has been expurgated from your temple and you have filled your temple with the Word of God, you need to make sure you maintain a lifestyle that is consistently pleasing to God. Don't be fooled to believe you are free forever. Satan knows our weaknesses and the unclean spirits can roam for years, looking to return home. Therefore, you must maintain your deliverance, as it will not happen automatically.

In the summer of 2014, I witnessed negative behavior patterns trying to return in my life. I was displeased, and I knew I could not allow the enemy to grab ahold of me again. Furthermore, I certainly did not want to end up in a condition that was characteristically seven times worse. So, the moment I saw signs of my past behaviors, I knew something had to be done. I delved head first into the Word of God. Hearing from God and allowing the Holy Spirit to minister to me led to my continued freedom and my *Breaking Chains Conference* that was held in September 2014, so other women could be free from the chains that bound them.

Listed below are seven steps for maintaining deliverance. Putting these steps into action will effectuate a consistently clean temple.

1. **Put on the whole armour of God,** as set forth in Ephesians 6:10-18. There are seven pieces of armour. The natural purpose of each will be explained in detail first, so the spiritual purpose can be better understood.

1. *Loins girt about with truth.*

Explanation- To prepare for battle, a Roman soldier put around his waist a very wide belt, which was the holder for other equipment. There was a loop, for example, for the different swords. Just as the soldier had his loin belt to put on every day to keep his armor together, we must apply the Word of God to our lives on a daily basis, or we will not be able to maintain our defenses. The belt was the first thing the soldier put on. Just as this is the first thing a Christian must put on. Much of the weaponry and protection depended on the belt being properly in place. If we do not use the Word of God as our belt of truth, we will have no foundation on which to base our warfare with the enemy. The belt held things in place where they needed to be. The truth of God's Word does the same for us.

2. *The breastplate of righteousness.*

Explanation- The breastplate was attached to the belt by leather thongs passed through rings on the bottom to keep it solidly attached. It was anchored to the belt, and it was above the belt. When you walk in the righteousness of God, it is a weapon of defense against all those slanderous accusations and outrageous strategies of the devil. The Bible declares that the heart of man is prone to be tempted, according to Matthew 26:41. We are righteous in God's sight because of what Jesus did for us.

3. *Feet shod with the preparation of the Gospel of peace.*

Explanation- Some historians credit footwear as one of the greatest reasons why the Roman army was so victorious over its enemies. The Roman soldier was equipped with footwear that had spikes on the soles, which provided them a strong enough stance and balance that gave them a superior posture in battle on hills and uneven terrain. Offensively, this peace will help us to stand with our feet planted firmly on the Word of God and stay there, unmoved by the devil's threats and lies. It will protect us when we walk through the rough places and keep us steady in the heat of a battle. It will keep our spiritual foes where they belong- under our feet.

4. *The shield of faith.*

Explanation- The Romans had a long, rectangular, knees-to-chin shield, which protected them from arrows and spears and could be knelt behind during an arrow barrage. In this verse, the Roman shield stands for the faith of the believer in the promises of God. The value of faith lies not in the person exercising it, but in the person whom the faith is in. Faith is something that all people possess and use every day. Romans 10:17 tells us that faith comes through hearing the Word of God. Knowing the Bible and the god of the Bible gives us greater faith. Remember it is God that fights for us, and He is an awesome protector.

5. *The helmet of salvation.*

Explanation- The Roman helmet had a chinstrap, a visor, and came down to cover the back and sides of the neck. A well-designed helmet will protect us from various angles of attack. The greatest battlefield is our minds. This is the area that the enemy wants to attack the most. One key area he wants to damage is our assurance of salvation. We must be on guard with what we let run free in our minds. Satan is very subtle in these areas. He has blinded the world, and he will do the same to the unsuspecting or careless Christian. We must have a clear mind to be discerning in all situations. This comes by immersing ourselves in God's Word and prayer.

6. *The sword of the Spirit, which is the Word of God.*

Explanation- Apostle Paul spoke of one of five different types of Roman swords. This one was a two-edged sword with the end turned upward. It inflicted much more damage than the other swords. Not only was it intended to kill, but also it could rip the enemy's insides to shreds. It only needed to penetrate the enemy a depth of two to three inches to mortally wound him. Our sword of the Spirit is the Word of God. When Satan tempted Jesus in the wilderness, Jesus quoted His Father's words and spoke them with authority. Consequently, each word was like a sword-blow to Satan's head! God has given us the authority to use His words because we are all ambassadors of Christ. God speaks with ultimate authority in the universe. He spoke and the universe came into being from nothing. When we speak God's Word according to His will, there is no power in the universe who can withstand it!

7. *Praying in the Spirit.*

Explanation- In verse 18, we are told to pray in the Spirit (that is, with the mind of Christ, with His heart and His priorities) in addition to wearing the full armor of God. We cannot neglect prayer, as it is the means by which we draw spiritual strength from God. Without prayer, without reliance upon God, our efforts at spiritual warfare are empty and futile. The full armor of God—truth, righteousness, the gospel, faith, salvation, the Word of God, and prayer—are the tools God has given us, through which we can be spiritually victorious, overcoming Satan's attacks and temptations.

2. **Refuse the thoughts demons give you** and replace them with spiritual thoughts. Apostle Paul gave us good advice in Philippians 4:8: *"Finally, brethren, whatsoever things are true, whatsoever things are honest, whatsoever things are just, whatsoever things are pure, whatsoever things are lovely, whatsoever things are of good report; if there be any virtue, and if there be any praise, think on these things."*

At times, thoughts will cross our minds that could easily lead us into sinful acts. First, we need not to be embarrassed about our thoughts. Having thoughts (good or evil) is not sinful. Second, entertaining the thought is what could possibly lead to sinful acts, if the acts are contrary to God's Word. II Corinthians 10:5 says, *"Casting down imaginations, and every high thing that exalteth itself against the knowledge of God, and bringing into captivity every thought to the obedience of Christ."* We can easily control our actions if we first control our thoughts. Things don't just happen. Every action begins with a thought. When those thoughts are entertained, eventually they lead to actions.

3. **Positive confession** is faith expressed. Negative confessions characterize demonic influence and will open the door to the

enemy (Mark 11:23). Jesus withstood Satan's temptations by using scripture. The Word is a mirror to the soul (James 1:22-25); it is a lamp unto the feet for guidance (Psalm 119:105); it is a cleansing agent (Eph. 5:25-26); it is a two-edged sword, laying bare the heart (Heb. 4:12); and it is food for the spirit (I Pet. 2:2 ; Matt. 4:4). No person can long maintain deliverance apart from the Word of God as a primary factor in his/her life (Psalm 1:1-3)!

Have you ever encountered a person who every time you saw him he only had something negative to say? Have you ever tried to combat his negativity with the Word of God, but he consistently refused to receive encouragement? How did you feel after you left his presence? The experience can be downright depressing! However, if we confess the Word over our lives, we will feel empowered, uplifted, and encouraged. When I have thoughts of a situation that isn't positive, I quickly shift my thoughts to the Word of God. Then, I open my mouth and begin to praise Him. A far better way to be positive and remain positive is to begin your day with praises unto God as soon as you open your eyes. This will set a positive precedent for your day.

4. **Take up your cross daily** and follow Jesus (Luke 9:23). If fleshly appetites, desires and lusts are not brought to the cross, a way for demons to return will be left open (Gal. 5:19-21, 24).

According to Evangelist Billy Graham, in Luke 9:23, Jesus was expressing to the disciples a life choice that was necessary for them to make. Graham (2006) stated,

In Jesus' day, a cross was a symbol of suffering, and we all have trials and afflictions that may be very hard for us to bear—even with God's help. But Jesus meant something far deeper than this when He told His disciples to carry their cross. In Jesus' day, a cross wasn't just a symbol of pain and suffering; it was mainly a symbol of death. What Jesus was telling them is that they needed to put to death their own plans and desires, and then turn their lives over to Him and do His will every day. You see, Jesus doesn't simply call us to believe that He existed, or even to believe that He can save us. He calls on us to commit our whole lives to Him— to trust Him alone for our salvation, and then to follow Him as His disciples. He said, *'Anyone who does not carry his cross and follow me cannot be my disciple'* (Luke 14:27). Is Christ the master of your life? Have you put to death your own plans and committed yourself to His will for your life? Don't be satisfied with anything less, for there is no greater joy in life than following Christ every day.

5. **Develop a life of continuous praise and prayer,** which silences the enemy. Pray in the Spirit (in tongues) and also in the understanding (in your native tongue) (I Cor. 14:14). Pray without ceasing (I Thess. 5:17).

To "pray without ceasing" refers to recurring prayer, not nonstop talking. Prayer is to be a way of life—you are to be continually in an attitude of prayer. It is living in continual God-consciousness, where everything you see and experience becomes a kind of prayer, lived in deep awareness of and surrender to Him. It should be instant and intimate communication-not unlike that which we enjoy with our best friend. To 'pray without ceasing' means when you are tempted, you hold the temptation before God and ask for

His help. When you experience something good and beautiful, you immediately thank the Lord for it. When you see evil around you, you ask God to make it right and to use you toward that end, if that is His will. When you meet someone who does not know Christ, you pray for God to draw that person to Himself and to use you to be a faithful witness. When you encounter trouble, you turn to God as your Deliverer. Thus, life becomes a continually ascending prayer: all life's thoughts, deeds, and circumstances become an opportunity to commune with your Heavenly Father. In that way you constantly set your mind *"on the things above, not on the things that are on earth"* (Colossians 3:2). (MacArthur, 1995, pp. 15-17)

6. **Maintain a life of fellowship and spiritual ministry**. It is the sheep that wander from the flock that are most endangered. Hebrews 10:25 warns us, *"Not forsaking the assembling of ourselves together, as the manner of some is; but exhorting one another: and so much the more, as ye see the day approaching."* When believers spend time together, they can encourage one another and share their concerns with each other. And, when one of the believers needs prayer, he/she has a family of believers who can intercede on his/her behalf. Remember, Proverbs 27:17 declares, *"As iron sharpens iron, so one person sharpens another"* (NIV).

In addition to maintaining fellowship with other believers, you should also desire spiritual gifts and yield to their operation through you within the body of Christ (I Cor. 12:7-14). The gifts and talents you have been given are to build the kingdom of God. God has entrusted us with various gifts, or abilities, that He expects us to use for His glory. I Corinthians 12:4-7 says, *"There are diversities of gifts, but the same Spirit. There are differences of ministries, but the same Lord. And there are diversities of activities, but it is the same God who works all in all. But the manifestation of the Spirit is given to each one for the profit of all."* Ephesians 4:11-13 says, *"And He Himself gave some to be apostles, some prophets, some evangelists, and some pastors and teachers, for the equipping of the saints for the work of ministry, for the edifying of the body of Christ, till we all come to the unity of the faith and of the knowledge of the Son of God, to a perfect man, to the measure of the stature of the fullness of Christ."* Whatever gift(s) you have been blessed with, use it/them to glorify the Lord and to build His kingdom.

7. Commit yourself totally to Christ. Determine that your every thought, word and action will reflect the very nature of Christ. Faith, trust in God, is the greatest weapon against the devil's lies (Eph. 6:16). James 4:7-10 says: *"Submit yourselves therefore to God. Resist the devil, and he will flee from you. Draw nigh to God, and he will draw nigh to you. Cleanse your hands, ye sinners; and purify your hearts, ye double minded. Be afflicted, and mourn, and weep: let your laughter be turned to mourning, and your joy to heaviness. Humble yourselves in the sight of the Lord, and he shall lift you up."*

Following these seven steps will ensure that your "house" (body) remains filled after having been cleansed. Staying filled will assist with remaining delivered and prevent the enemy from returning. Do not settle for anything less (Romans 5:10)!

Chapter 6
Closing Thoughts

When God created Adam and Eve and placed them in the Garden of Eden, everything they needed was at their disposal. God had only one requirement: for them to refrain from eating from the tree of the knowledge of good and evil. God warned if they were to be disobedient and eat from the tree, they would surely die the same day (Genesis 2:17). As we continue reading, we find out Adam and Eve disobeyed God, and as God had promised, they experienced spiritual death: They were immediately disconnected from God and consequently exiled from the garden.

With Adam's action of disobedience, sin, for the first time, entered into the world system (Romans 5:12). From that point forward, with the birth of their first child Cain, all of mankind was born into sin and shaped in iniquity (Psalm 51:5). So, due to the fall of man from God's graces, Satan was given a measure of power. However, Satan cannot do anything without God's permission, as seen in the book of Job. Furthermore, Satan cannot do anything to us without our express permission. When we commit sin and remove ourselves from God's divine protection, we thereby give Satan permission to attack us. Hence, we give Satan the right-of-way to send unclean spirits to dwell in our temple and wreak havoc in our lives.

At the same time, we must be clear about who we are and whose we are as believers. Hebrews 2:6-7 says, *"But there is a place where someone has testified: "What is mankind that you are mindful of them, a son of man that you care for him? You made them a little lower than the angels; you crowned them with glory and honor"* (NIV). The angels are the heavenly hosts and are blessed to be in the presence of God continually. They must be very special to God in order for Him to allow them in His company on a regular and permanent basis.

Think for a moment about your regular dwelling place-your home. Are you particular about who comes to visit or to sleep over? I know I am. Like me, most people view their home as a sacred place, and it is usually only inhabited by family and close friends. Of course, the occasional stranger or acquaintance may come by, but the stranger doesn't usually stay for an extended period of time.

Because God sees us a little lower than the angels, He holds us in high esteem. We are His creation. He loves us dearly (John 3:16). Therefore, it logically follows that He wants the best for us. Also, the Word says in I Peter 2:9, *"But you are a chosen people, a royal priesthood, a holy nation, God's special possession, that you may declare the praises of him who called you out of darkness into his wonderful light"* (NIV). God sees us as royalty, so we should not settle for second best, and we must not take a back seat to the enemy, giving him the right-of-way in our lives. We should not forfeit our God-given authority or privileges to the enemy.

Instead, we should adorn ourselves with the whole armor of God, as discussed in detail in Chapter Five and walk tall and mighty, being strong in the Lord (Ephesians 6:10). And, we should do so without fear, for the Lord has not given us the spirit of fear, but of power, love, and a sound mind (I Timothy 1:7). If we trust God and use the tools He has provided for us, He will stand with us and He will honor His Word in Isaiah 43:19 that says, *"Behold, I will do a new thing; now it shall spring forth; shall ye not know it? I will even make a way in the wilderness, and rivers in the desert."*

Now that we have a clear understanding of 1) how unclean spirits can be given the right-of-way to enter into our lives due to our sin nature, 2) how to get rid of the unclean spirits, and 3) how to stay clean, we must also understand that ultimately, we have the power to decide and determine what will happen in our individual lives. We can be bound by the enemy and remain bound, or we can be set free in the name of our Lord and Savior Jesus Christ and only submit to Jesus as His bondservant (one who willingly submits to the service of another). Remember, Jesus has given us the power to tread on serpents and scorpions, and nothing by any means shall harm us (Luke 10:19). However, most assuredly harm *will* come if we allow spiritual doors to be opened and to remain open. But if we close the doors to the enemy, we remove the possibility of harm.

The Word of God says, *"My people are destroyed for lack of knowledge"* (Hosea 4:6). Now that you have the knowledge, and you know how to deal with unclean spirits, utilize your God-given power to be set free today in the name of Jesus.

Once you are set free from unclean spirits, you will be more effective in your service to the Lord. You can work unencumbered. If you have not already begun to serve God or if you are looking to expand your service, listed below are fifteen different ways to serve God through serving others.

1. Serve God through serving your family (Ephesians 6:2; I Timothy 5:8).
2. Give tithes and offerings (for the furtherance of ministry) (Malachi 3:8-10).
3. Volunteer in your community (Matthew 25:40).
4. Care for the sick and shut-in (James 5:13-15).
5. Donate clothing and food (James 1:27).
6. Be a friend (John 15:12-15)
7. Serve children (James 1:27).
8. Assist those in mourning (II Corinthians 1:3-4).
9. Share your talents (Matthew 25:14-30).
10. Simple acts of kindness (find a need and fill it).
11. Missionary work (Matthew 28:19).
12. Fulfill your callings (II Timothy 1:6).
13. Use your creativity.
14. Humble yourself (I Peter 5:6).
15. Submit yourself as a willing vessel unto the Lord (II Timothy 2:20-22).

There is much work in God's kingdom for each of us to do. As soon as you feel equipped, get started. Remember, only attempt to do what God has called you to do. Refrain from trying to do someone else's job because you *think* you are equipped or because it looks glamorous or has prestige. You will only be truly successful in what God has called you to do.

In closing, let us pray.

Dear Heavenly Father,

We approach your throne of grace with all humility and reverence that is due unto you. Father, we ask that you forgive us of all our sins committed covertly and overtly. Father God, you know our hearts. We come to you in the spirit of repentance, asking for you to cleanse us from all impurity. Oh Father God, allow us to walk in righteousness. We know we are not righteous through any good of our own but because of the shed blood of Jesus Christ. Father God, we commit our lives to serving you. And as we encounter the many distractions and temptations that surround us, Father, we ask that you would give us the strength to endure, the strength to overcome, the strength to be strong, the strength to walk in peace, and the strength to walk in the spirit of the Lord. We take upon ourselves the responsibility to study your Word and to develop a relationship with you to draw forever nigh unto you God because we know that in you there is strength, we know that in you there is power, and we know that in you we are over comers, as we are victors in Christ Jesus.

Father, it is our desire to live a life that is pleasing unto you and to be a sweet smelling savor unto your nostrils. Lord, you called us out of darkness and into your marvelous light. We are the salt of the world that you called us to be, and we desire to bring glory and honor to your name. Lord, make every crooked path straight and keep us from the snare of the fowler and the noisome pestilence. Oh Lord, give us strength for the journey and order each and every one of our steps. Father, we thank you for each and every blessing that you have bestowed upon us and for every provision. Lord, continue to shelter us and to be our strong tower. Give us wisdom as we march forward in our service to you.

Father, we ask that you receive this prayer in the name of our Lord and Savior Jesus Christ.

Amen!

References:

Graham, B. (2006). Billy Graham Evangelistic Association. billygraham.org

Hayford, Jack W. (2011). How and Why We Worship. Jack Hayford Ministries. jackhayford.org.

MacArthur, J. (1995). *Alone with God.* Publisher: David C. Cook. pp. 15-17.

Gift of Salvation
for Non-Believers

"For all have sinned, and come short of the glory of God."
Romans 3:23

This section was written especially for non-believers, those who have not accepted the gift of salvation. The gift of salvation saves souls from eternal dam-nation and is a free gift offered by God himself.

John 3:16-18 says, *"For God so loved the world, that he gave his only begotten Son, that whosoever believeth in him should not perish, but have everlasting life. For God sent not his Son into the world to condemn the world; but that the world through him might be saved. He that believeth on him is not condemned: but he that believeth not is condemned already, because he hath not believed in the name of the only begotten Son of God."*

This section of scripture tells us God's purpose for giving His son Jesus to the world. The world was in a bad condition. The world was overwrought with sin; the people were living for fleshly desires rather than for God's desires.

As a result of the world's conditions, God decided that He would offer the perfect sacrifice that would save the world from being a place where people were lost and had no hope. He decided that His own son could stand in proxy for the sin-filled world, taking all sin upon Himself.

So Jesus came, born of a virgin, to save this dying world. He walked on this earth for 33 ½ years, doing the work of His Heavenly Father. At the appointed time, He died by way of crucifixion upon a cross at Calvary, on Golgatha's hill. He shed his blood and died for you and for me. Because His blood was pure, it paid the penalty for all unrighteousness and gave those who believe in Him direct access to His father's throne.

Scripture tells us in Matthew 27:51 that the veil of the temple was ripped in two from top to bottom, at the moment that Jesus' spirit left His body. As a result of the veil's removal, we are no longer required to have a high priest make intercession for us. We, as the children of the Most High God, are able to approach the throne God for ourselves, and Jesus sits on the right hand of the Father making intercession for us.

But what is even more miraculous than God offering His own son as the perfect sacrifice was the fact that when Jesus was placed in grave clothes and placed in a tomb, He only remained there until the third day. God would not have it that His son would remain in the heart of the earth forever. In order for people to believe in the awesome power of God and His dear son Jesus, a miracle had to be performed. So, on the third day, after Jesus died on the cross, He was resurrected, demonstrating the omnipotence of God. This very act was the act that would cause people to believe in a god that reigns supreme and holds the power of the universe in His very hands, a god that could save them from themselves.

Today, if you are an unbeliever, you can change your destiny. You can change where you will spend your eternity. Our Heavenly Father gives us the freedom of choice about how we want to live our life here on earth and how we want to spend eternity. In Deuteronomy 30:19, God boldly declares, "*I call heaven and earth to record this day against you, that I have set before you life and death, blessing and cursing: therefore choose life, that both thou and thy seed may live.*"

So, dear friend what choice will you make today? Will you spend your eternity with the Creator or will you suffer Hell's eternal flames? Again, the choice is yours. Just as the men aboard the ship who were with Jonah became believers, you too can make a choice to accept the only one and true living God as your god.

If after reading the above passages, you have decided that you want to spend your eternity in Heaven with God, the creator, and His son Jesus, and the Holy Spirit, read through what has affectionately come to be known as the Roman's Road. This is the road to salvation. As you read through the scriptures that comprise the Roman's Road, you will also read the explanation for each scripture so you will have clarity about what you are reading and confessing.

The Roman's Road to Salvation

The road to salvation begins with Romans 3:23 which declares, "*For all have sinned, and come short of the glory of God.*" This scripture explains that everyone has come short of God's glory and needs redemption. Then Romans 6:23a states, "*For the wages of sin is death.*" Here, we learn that the consequence of living a life of sin is death. Everyone will experience physical death as a result of the sin committed in the garden of Eden, but those who commit themselves to a life of sin will suffer eternal damnation in the lake of fire (Rev. 19).

Continue with the rest of verse 6:23 that says, "*but the gift of God is eternal life through Jesus Christ our Lord.*" There is an alternative to suffering eternal damnation. We can accept the gift of salvation by accepting Jesus as our personal lord and savior. Then, Romans 5:8 says, "*But God commendeth his love toward us, in that, while we were yet sinners, Christ died for us.*" We are able to receive the gift of salvation because Christ came to earth and shed His blood for us on the cross.

Continue to Romans 10: 9-10 which says, "*That if thou shalt confess with thy mouth the Lord Jesus, and shalt believe in thine heart that God hath raised him from the dead, thou shalt be saved. For with the heart man believeth unto righteousness; and with the mouth confession is made unto salvation.*" If we confess with our mouths that Jesus is the son of God, that he came and died for our sins, and that God raised Him from the dead, we will receive salvation.

Finish with Romans 10:13, which states, "*For whosoever shall call upon the name of the Lord shall be saved.*" Call upon the name of God by saying these words, "**Lord Jesus, come into my heart and save me Lord. I believe that you are the Son of God who came and died on the cross for my sins. I believe that you rose from the grave. I also believe that you now sit in heaven on the right side of the Father, making intersession for me. I accept you as my Lord and my Savior.**"

Now that you have confessed with your mouth that Jesus is the son of God and that He died for our sins and rose from the grave, **YOU ARE NOW SAVED!!!!** You will spend your eternity in heaven.

The next step is very important- you must find a Bible-based church that teaches the Word of God and confesses the Lord Jesus Christ to be the son of God. Don't delay. Do this immediately. Do not leave yourself open to the enemy. Get connected with the saints of the Most High God and keep yourself covered with the unspotted blood of the lamb.

Here is my prayer for you.
Father God,

I thank you for the opportunity to minister your word to the unsaved, the unchurched, and the uncommitted. Father God, I pray now for the souls who have just received the gift of salvation. Lord Father, they have opened their hearts to you, and I know that you have received them into your kingdom and written their names in the Book of Life. Father God, I pray that you will touch their lives and show yourself mightily before them. Let their eyes be opened by the scales falling off, allowing them to see clearly.

Father God, I even pray for the backslider, those who have turned away from you after receiving the gift of salvation. You said in your word that you desire that none would perish. So Lord, I send your word to them right now praying that they would confess the iniquity in their heart, repent, and turn from their evil ways, so that they may receive a life of abundance. You said in your word in Matthew Chapter 14, that every knee shall bow before you and every tongue will confess that Jesus is Lord.

Father God, I pray now that we all come under subjection to your word and that we will humbly submit our lives to you. I ask all these things in the name of my Lord and Savior Jesus Christ.

Amen, Amen, Amen!!!!

I will continue to pray for your success in your walk with God. Remember, this spiritual walk that you are about to embark on will not be an easy walk, but remember, the race is not given to the swift but to those who endure to the end.

Be blessed with heaven's best. I love you!

OTHER BOOKS

BY THE AUTHOR

(All books can be purchased at

www.creativemindsbookstore or amazon.com)

From Despair, through Determination, to Victory!

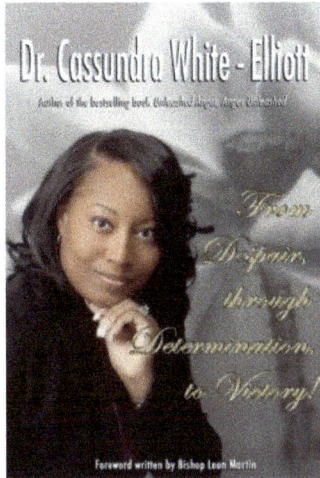

A lot can happen during a span of 40 years. The life of Dr. Cassundra White-Elliott has been anything but uneventful. From a fun-loving childhood sprinkled with incidents of abuse to a tumultuous young adulthood to a stable, secure adult life, she has experienced a full life, with much more to come. Her story is inspiring and motivating.

If anyone lacks hope, reading Dr. White-Elliott's autobiography will propel him/her into an attitude of "Maybe I can." This attitude, if nurtured and developed, will grow into an attitude of "Yes, I can." Throughout her life, Cassundra has always held in her heart the belief that she could achieve anything that she had a made-up mind to embark upon. She was determined to achieve her heart's desires, doing what God has called her to do. She takes no credit for herself. All the glory goes to God, for He is her driving force. In Him, she lives, moves, and has her being.

Through the Storm

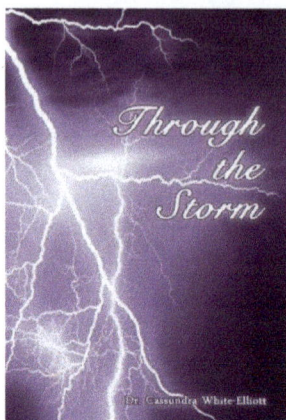

Through the Storm was duly inspired by the avaricious cloud of depression that decided to hover overhead of my daily existence in the latter part of 2007. Although I found it extremely difficult, I was once again compelled to not be defeated by just another snare that the enemy, the trickster, set for me. Once again, or more appropriately I should say *continuously*, he has exerted pernicious efforts to snatch the very life out of me by causing me to wallow in despair and to believe that I had been overcome by failure when in actuality and all reality, I was just experiencing a temporary setback. During those cloudy days, I had to remind myself daily that even though I was a target of the enemy, I am and will always be a child of the Most High god, Jehovah, who is my rock, my stability.

Public Speaking in the Spiritual Arena

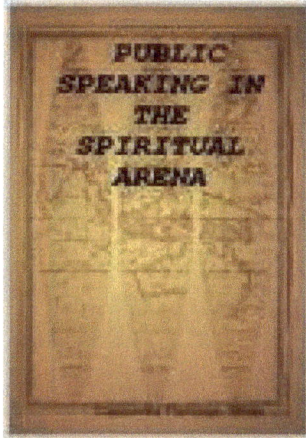

Gain the tools to speak successfully in public, with particular focus on the spiritual arena.

Where is Your Joppa?

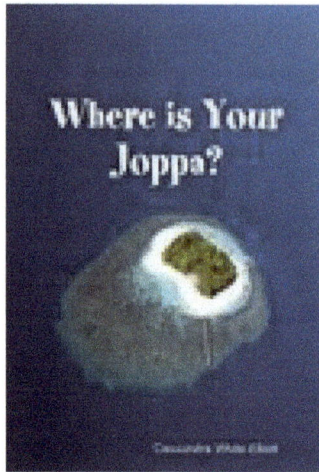

Where is Your Joppa? was written for the express purpose of illustrating God's call for obedience in the lives of believers with respect to the individual call that He has on each of our lives. As you read throughout the various chapters, notice that the emphasis is placed on our persistent disobedience in answering God's call in a specific area of our lives. We have become a people who are similar to the Israelites when they found themselves in the middle of the wilderness, following their exodus from Egypt. Before God, they murmured and complained about their current life conditions and failed to be obedient to God's statutes delivered through His servant Moses. Their persistent disobedience caused them to lose the opportunity to see and enter the Promised Land. I ask you, "What has your disobedience cost you?" "Was your disobedience worth what it cost you?"

Mayhem in the Hamptons

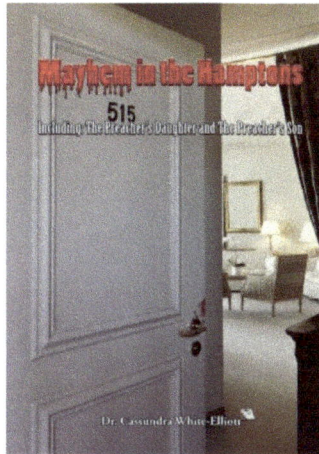

Romero and Yolanda optimistically plan for the day that is going to change their lives from being single persons to a couple who is united in holy matrimony. They, along with their parents, close friends and family, fly over to the infamous Hamptons, where only the rich and famous vacation, to have their dream wedding at the five-star Hampton Suites located on a peninsula in the Hamptons. Little do they know that their perfect day will turn out to be less than perfect when their wedding planner Mariesha Coleman suddenly goes missing!

Mayhem in the Hamptons is a tale that shares how the horrors of a woman's past can come back to haunt her in more than one way and the impact it can have on anyone who gets in the way.

The Preacher's Daughter

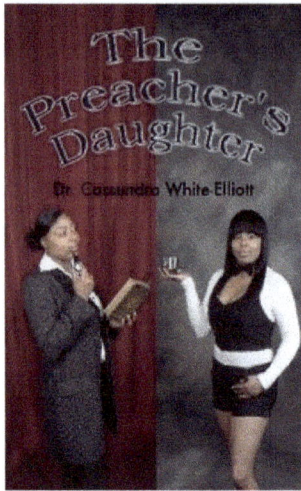

Tinisha, the daughter of a preacher, is a twenty-six year old God-fearing young woman endeavoring to complete law school so that she can make her mark in the courtroom. Working in one of the late-night clubs in Hollywood to earn money to pay her own way through school, Tinisha soon learns that life doesn't always go as planned. Finding her strength in her faith, Tinisha constantly finds herself praying as she watches God move miraculously in her life.

Preacher's Son

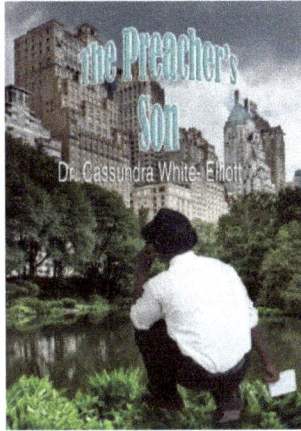

Romero Turner is a private investigator with a promising future. As he continues to build his career, he is excited about the cases he undertakes. However, his father Pastor Theodore Turner has other plans for his son's life. In the midst of trying to save his client's husband from Sylvester Domingo, a ruthless crime lord, Romero must try to salvage his relationship with his father. He must decide if ministry or life as a detective is in his future.

Lord, Teach Me to be a Blessing!

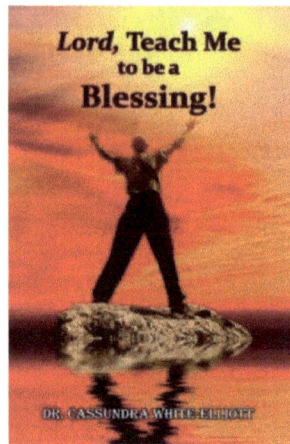

Lord, Teach Me to be a Blessing! will change a person's mentality from being centered around "me, myself, and I" to focusing on "others." The world system teaches us that it is acceptable to place ourselves above others in an attempt to get ahead and even to survive. Herbert Spencer coined the phrase *'survival of the fittest'* after reading Charles Darwin's theory of evolution. This concept of surpassing and outdoing others is the world's philosophy. However, the Word of God does not subscribe to or promote this self-centered ideology, and therefore, neither should believers. We must hold fast to the truths outlined in Holy Scripture: "*Love thy neighbor as you love thyself*" (James 2:8) and "*It is more blessed to give than to receive*" (Acts 20:35).

While holding God's truths to be self-evident, we must demonstrate them to others, thereby showing them the way of the Lord of how to be a blessing to someone *rather* than looking to receive a blessing.

After the Dust Settles

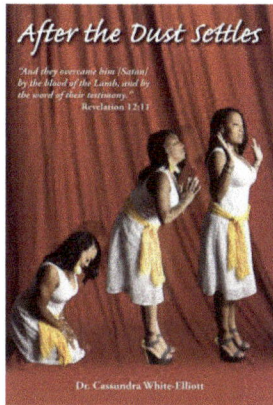

Throughout the journey of life, we all experience ups and downs and joys and pains. Most of us successfully find solutions to the situations/problems we encounter, but we often avoid dealing with the attached emotions. If we continue to ignore the emotions of pain, hurt, disappointment, anger, etc., we set ourselves up for destruction. Our families, our cultures, and our society tell us to be strong, to keep our chin up, and to grin and bear it. However, these methods of avoidance can lead us to strokes due to the undue amount of pressure we place on ourselves and/or mental illness from being unable to cope with the emotional baggage we have accumulated.

In *After the Dust Settles*, Dr. C. White-Elliott shares several situations that we all may encounter at one time or another in our lifetime and how to successfully navigate through them, so we can find ourselves emotionally healthy after the dust has settled and the situation has been rectified.

A Diamond in the Rough

A Diamond in the Rough Architecture Firm was built and is owned and operated by lead architect Kyra Fraser. For the last five years, Kyra has been extremely successful in business, but her love life leaves much to be desired.

Kyra has set high standards for herself and does not wish to take a man in any condition and attempt to make him over. She is looking for someone who is drama free, well educated, very cultured, fun-loving, good looking, self-motivated, and the list goes on.

Will Kyra find the man of her dreams, or will her dream just continue to be a dream?

As you delve into this page-turning novel, Kyra's reality will unfold as you are drawn into her world of design, love and office drama-which includes her best friend's husband who is looking for love in all the wrong places.

365 Days of Encouragement

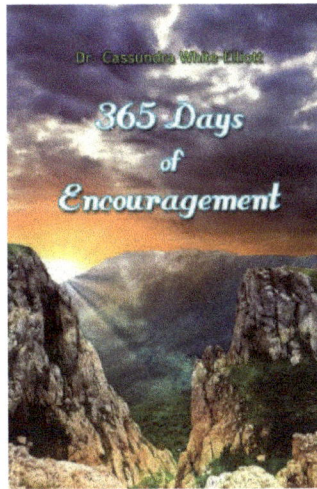

Just as our brain requires oxygen obtained from the air we breathe to sustain our mortal bodies, our spirit requires revitalization and encouragement in order to be strengthened each and every day of our lives. The revitalization and encouragement needed for the spirit of man comes directly from the Word of God and assists us in walking according to the way of our heavenly Father. *365 Days of Encouragement* provides a scripture a day for each day of the year. Along with the daily scripture is a brief note of commentary also for the benefit of edifying the saints of God. It is my prayer that the people of God would live a fulfilled life through Christ Jesus. Knowing His word and understanding we can walk in the fulfillment thereof is empowering. We are instructed in II Timothy 2:15, "Study to shew thyself approved unto God, a workman that needeth not to be ashamed, rightly dividing the word of truth" (KJV).

A Mother's Heart

A Mother's Heart shares the unconditional love of mothers through a compilation of testimonies. Each testimony serves as a tribute to a special mother. The children of the represented mothers have lovingly written about their childhood, young adult life and/or older adult experiences they shared with their mother. As you read the writers' reflections, you will feel the expressions of love exude from the pages.

The purpose of this book is two-fold. First, it honors those mothers who stood by their children through the trials of life and showered them with unconditional love. Second, the book is a source of encouragement for mothers who may feel inadequate and question whether or not they are actually suited for motherhood.

Mothers may not be perfect, but they are definitely unmatched by any other category of person on God's green earth!

Power of a Woman

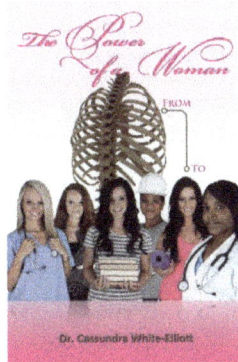

The ongoing conversation about the value of a woman is presented from a different perspective in ***The Power of a Woman***. Dr. Cassundra White-Elliott presents a biblical perspective of women and compares it to the worldview of both yesterday and today. This comparison seeks to illustrate God's intended purpose for His uniquely designed creation: *woman*. Dr. Elliott shares God's truth about pre-imposed limitations set by man versus the limitations God Himself set for woman in addition to the wealth of liberality He gave her.

Women's creativity and abilities are not meant to be stifled. They are meant to be utilized to bring glory to God, to help sustain and nurture their families, and to move the world forward. Knowing God's truth will show women how to celebrate and appreciate who they are as well as one another!

Women, let's take the blinders off, lift our heads up, and march forward, side by side with men, and bring glory and honor to God! Take your rightful place with a gentle smile and grace and be who God called you to be!

A Touch in the Dark

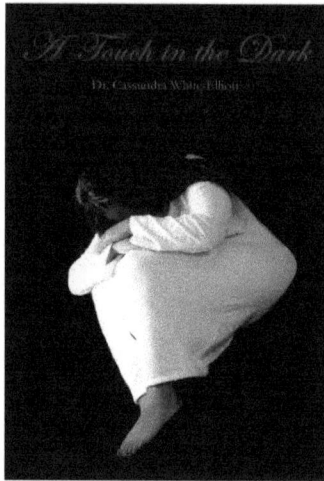

Dr. Teri Langston is enjoying life with her husband Reggie and doing all that she loves to do: traveling, eating good food, spending time with family and friends, and re-decorating her home. Her career is doing well, and life is grand. In her world, there is nothing else that she needs- except a little healing. From the recesses of her mind, her past sneaks back in to haunt her and remind her of traumatic events she once endured. In the midst of living fantasies fulfilled, Teri finds herself grasping for peace in the middle of a still, quiet storm. Surrounded by her loving family, Teri wonders if the memories will ever fade, if the uncomfortable feelings will ever subside, and if she will ever turn the past loose. Take this journey with Teri as she laughs, cries, rejoices, and looks for answers. Will she find the peace she longs for or will her suffering be prolonged?

Broken Chains

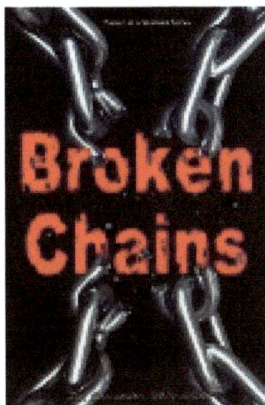

Broken Chains is an in-depth survey of five life-changing tragedies that can and will serve as chains to bind us if we are not watchful and mindful of their potential effects. In our lifetimes, we may all experience death of loved ones, sexual abuse, broken relationships, promiscuity, and sickness and disease. These everyday life occurrences can have detrimental effects on the remaining years of our lives and change our existence, unless we deal with them in a healthy manner.

Broken Chains not only brings to light the detrimental effects of five life-changing tragedies, but it also shares how anyone who experiences them can be healed and delivered from their effects.

If you have experienced death of a loved one, sexual abuse, a broken relationship, the effects of promiscuity, and/or sickness and disease and have not been able to rid yourself of the emotions attached to them or specific resulting behaviors, **Broken Chains** is for you. God designed each of us for a purpose, and He has an intended end for us to achieve. In order for us to effectively achieve our God-given purpose, we must be free of chains that bind us. It is not God's desire that we become immobilized by life's events. His desire is for us to be healed, delivered and set free. Be healed today, in the name of the Lord Jesus Christ!

I Have Fallen

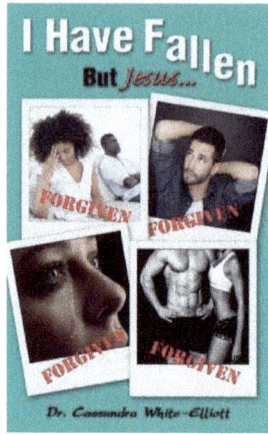

Do you know anyone who has committed his/her life to Christ but has done something unseemly that you would never expect a Christian to do? How did you feel about that person or what the person did? Did you pass judgment? What if that person were you? How would you feel if you made a misstep and no one forgave you and instead began to treat you differently? How do you feel when you are judged for past mistakes or lifestyles that are no longer part of your life?

This book shares four true stories of Christians who have made missteps during their walk with God. The purpose is not to air their dirty laundry, but to demonstrate our humanness and our vulnerability. None of us are exempt from making errors and falling into sin. It can happen to any of us.

The solution for these dilemmas is for the person who fell into sin to make a life-changing move and turn away from the sin, repent and ask God for forgiveness. His arms are waiting!

The next solution is for those who witness the sin or know of it. Pray and be of comfort to the one who has fallen. Lead him/her back to the path of righteousness. Love thy neighbor and treat him/her as you want to be treated!

Fear Not

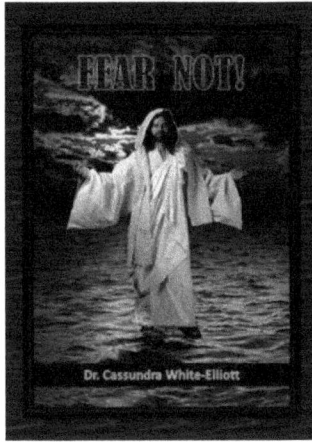

Fear affects people on a daily basis. It can prevent them from opening up and sharing their most heartfelt emotions, trying a new activity, achieving their dream, meeting new people, attaining desired accomplishments, going back to school, etc.

2 Timothy 1:7 declares, *"For God hath not given us the spirit of fear; but of power, and of love, and of a sound mind."*

The Bottom Line

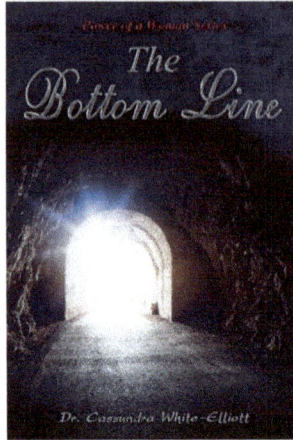

The Bottom Line is a detailed review of the Book of Job. Much can be said about Job's experiences with the loss of his children and wealth and the subsequent return of it all in mass proportions. However, the telling of Job's story in the Holy writ was not intended to focus on the return of his wealth. Instead, the focal point should be on the *bottom line* of the entire situation.

When you experience trials or tragedies in your life, do you tend to focus on the trial itself, the result, or the *bottom line*?

"What is the *bottom line*?" you may ask. The *bottom line* is the message God is sending regarding the situation.

When Job experienced his tragedies, there was a *bottom line*. Likewise, when you experience your trials and tragedies, there is a *bottom line* as well. It is up to you to discover it.

This book will reveal the *bottom line* in the Book of Job. It is readily apparent, but many often overlook it.

Now, it is up to you to uncover the *bottom line* of your experiences, for God will not bring a trial to you without a good reason.

ABOUT THE AUTHOR

Dr. Cassundra White-Elliott resides in California with her family, where as an English/Education professor she works for various community colleges and universities.

When writing, she writes with the direction of the Holy Spirit, in an effort to share with God's people all that He has for them.

In addition to teaching and writing, Dr. White-Elliott also serves as an evangelistic teacher. She is also the founder of International Women's Commission, a ministry that serves the needs of the entire person, by attending to healing the mind, body, soul, and spirit.

Dr. White-Elliott holds a Ph.D. in Education, a Master's in English Composition, and a Bachelor's in Education.

Dr. White-Elliott is also the founder of CLF Publishing, LLC. For your publishing needs, go online to www.clfpublishing.org.

www.ingramcontent.com/pod-product-compliance
Lightning Source LLC
Chambersburg PA
CBHW040419110426
42813CB00013B/2699